Unlocking Love is more than a book, it's a journey [illegible] brave woman willing to share her experiences [illegible] story breeds connection, and I love how I was able to [illegible] emotions of Stacey through her words. This is a life journey put on paper, and I encourage anyone to read this, but especially young women who want to grow and learn how to experience true love, God's love. Thank you, Stacey, for this masterpiece!

—DEVON DANIEL, Executive Pastor and author of *The Purposeful Parent: Your Calling Behind Parenthood*

From the first paragraph, reading *Unlocking Love* by Stacey Szczepanski feels like sitting down to hear a shocking story from a best friend. Her transparency and vulnerability immediately takes you on an emotional roller coaster with her in real-time . . . then unfolds into a relatable journey of unraveling her inner dialogue and unlocking the truest version of herself that has been waiting to break free all along. Anyone who has experienced the pressures of not settling for the wrong partner or simply struggled to fully embrace themselves in the present moment will be encouraged by Stacey's story!

—SARA GONZALEZ, host of *Space & Purpose* podcast

From the first chapter to the last, Stacey takes you through the emotional pain, along with her vulnerability and romantic ideals, to the grounded reality, while emphasizing her never-wavering faith. Her intention in sharing her story is to document her healing journey, while helping others with their own, similar experiences.

—MICHELLE QUARTON, life coach and clinical therapist

Unlocking Love is a captivating story about how manipulation and self-doubt can turn into a beautiful journey of healing and hope. Through Stacey's experiences, she reminds us that we are enough, no matter what has happened in our past. It is a beautifully written, honest account of searching for true love, realizing that someone else will not bring us happiness, and empowering us to love ourselves. Through her examples of forgiveness, bravery, and faith, Stacey shows us that all of us are worthy of God's unwavering love. This book is thoughtful, engaging, and reflective, giving the reader a sense that they are not alone. If you've ever wondered how you can start living your most authentic life, with God at the center, this book is for you!

—MELISSA BENOIT, high school teacher, fellow single woman, and friend

The sharing of personal stories is an act of bravery. I am in awe of the courage it took for Stacey to tell hers. It's a harrowing one and vulnerable. It's a story of heartbreak and betrayal. But, more than anything, hers is a story of hope, resilience, and finding true worth in Jesus. She tells of the very good news that our value isn't found in what we've done or what was done to us, but in the One who delights in us and calls us "beloved."

—SUSIE FINKBEINER, author of *The All-American*

As a therapist and dad of two girls, this book terrified me! Stacey exposes a new realm for predatory behavior that all of us need to be paying attention to. The story pushes readers to root for Stacey, resist a desire to throttle her deceiver, all while marveling at a young woman's pursuit of a simple goodness in her life—love. Her trusted companion, riding shotgun through all of it, is God. This book is like having coffee with an old friend, maybe with a shot of espresso! If half of us had her moxie and optimism for a good life, the world might just be okay!

—CHRIS KENWARD, LMSW, pediatric clinical social worker

Stacey Szczepanski has written a book that all victims of relationship trauma should read. She's experienced it all—catfishing, betrayal, guilt, remorse—and has emerged with vibrant faith, amazing strength, and a heart for those who are facing similar traumas. Her book will help you navigate your own relationships and regrets, and Stacey will become a trusted guide through her words and heart.

—ANN BYLE, author of *Chicken Scratch: Lessons on Living Creatively from a Flock of Hens*

UNLOCKING Love

UNLOCKING *Love*

How Being Catfished Deepened My Faith and Led Me on a Journey to Wholeness

STACEY SZCZEPANSKI

Unlocking Love

Published in the United States of America by Credo House Publishers,
a division of Credo Communications LLC, Grand Rapids, Michigan
credohousepublishers.com

ISBN: 978-1-62586-257-0

Cover and interior design by Sharon Van Loozenoord
Cover photo by Casey Camfferman
Editing by Donna Huisjen

Printed in the United States of America
First Edition

To all those who have been part of my story—
Thank you for growing me
in areas in which I didn't know I needed growth
and for being by my side through the tears, joys,
and the penny moments.

To all those who are about to read my story—
Thank you for being kind, compassionate, and understanding
as you journey through some of my most vulnerable moments
and are blessed with discovering some of your own.

To all the trials and triumphs God has led me through—
Thank you for revealing more of who He has created me to be.

CONTENTS

FOREWORD | xi

INTRODUCTION: Telling My Story | xv

PART 1: The Event

1 June 27, 2016—Freedom Day | 1

2 What Shapes You? | 7

3 Going Fishing | 15

4 The Fish Is Set Free | 33

PART 2: Slow Rebuild

5 Time to Rebuild | 45

6 Rejection. Grief. Memories. | 53

7 Relationships after Trauma | 61

8 What You're Never Told about Love | 75

9 The Importance of Communication | 87

10 The End Is Near | 103

PART 3: Discovering My Identity

11 The Journey Back to Him | 117

12 You Have to Start Somewhere | 131

13 Post-Traumatic Growth (PTG) is Continuous Work . . . Keep Going | 141

14 Discover, Forgive, and Comfort Your Inner Child | 155

15 Embrace Every Moment | 167

16 Unlocking Your True Self | 179

EPILOGUE: Releasing My Story | 193

RESOURCES | 205

ACKNOWLEDGMENTS | 207

ABOUT THE AUTHOR | 209

FOREWORD

Michelle Quarton, Life Coach

> "The wounded mind must be reset like a fractured bone.
> It cannot heal itself without spiritual realignment."
>
> —ANTHON ST. MAARTEN

Unlocking Love is a true and transparent, detailed account of the complex psychological, emotional, and physical trauma that co-occur with catfishing. This book is also a recording of the author's journey from trauma to self-awareness and post-traumatic growth.

In the March, 2023, article *Computers and Human Behavior*, Science Direct defines catfishing as "a form of online deception and fraud, whereby an individual steals the identity of another person or creates a fake identity and uses this stolen/fake identity as their own. Catfishing is performed with the intent of tricking someone into developing an online relationship, making the act distinct from impersonation alone." While empirical data is unavailable at this time, over the past twenty years catfishing incidents have been well documented in the media, with victims experiencing mental health disturbances such as severe depression; anxiety; trauma; and, in extreme cases, death by suicide.

Stacey Szczepanski holds nothing back in sharing her journey of being "consciously catfished" to discovering her true love of self, Jesus, and others.

I have been a life coach and clinical therapist for more than thirty years, helping people navigate life while achieving their goals. I do not advertise my practice, yet clients come my way, referred by former clients. Seven years ago, Stacey was given my number by her close friend at a time when she was facing unimaginable betrayal and a volcano of devastating emotions when she realized she had been catfished over a period of seven years. Due to the crisis mode Stacey presented, I veered away from the typical introductions and paperwork of a first session and greeted her with a hug; as she cried, she began recounting details of the traumatic events leading up to this first meeting. Stacey explained the complex catfishing scam she'd been subjected to, along with her realization and tenuous acceptance of the scam only forty-eight hours before our meeting. Thus began our work together in developing a solid plan for moving forward.

Stacey's journey will take you through the evolution of the scam, the players involved, post-catfished relationships, and her healing and post-traumatic growth. It is essential for the reader to understand that post-traumatic growth (PTG) is defined as a positive psychological change experienced as a result of struggling with highly challenging and stressful life circumstances.

Stacey's skill as a teacher, literacy coach, and writer—supported by her faith and courage to share specific and intimate details of her relationship with the scammer, alongside her years of emotional and therapeutic work—offers a clear understanding of the roller coaster of emotional-relationship experiences, while guiding the reader through opportunities to pause and reflect. The relevant resources she includes are an added bonus.

From the first chapter to the last, Stacey takes you through the emotional pain, along with her vulnerability and romantic ideals, to the grounded reality, while emphasizing her never wavering faith. Her intention in sharing her story is to document her healing journey, while helping others with their own, similar experiences.

Over these years Stacey and I have worked together through her trauma and post-traumatic growth, setting and accomplishing her goals, both personally and professionally. Her source of strength has been her faith, with God as her rudder.

I have been a witness to Stacey's transformation through her trauma recovery, her renewed self-esteem, and the blossoming confidence and joy she chooses to experience in her everyday life. If you are struggling in a similar circumstance, or know someone else who is, encourage them to read Stacey's story to know they are not alone. There is a good life on the other side of trauma.

> "Bad things do happen. How I respond to them defines my character and the quality of my life. I can choose to sit in perpetual sadness, immobilized by the gravity of my loss, or I can choose to rise from the pain and treasure the most precious gift I have—life itself."
>
> —WALTER ANDERSON

INTRODUCTION

Telling My Story

LET'S FACE IT. Anyone can create a façade. Social media, for many, is that façade. Anyone you pass on the street, stand next to at the grocery store, or even connect with daily in some way can create a façade. A façade is like a mask that is put on to cover up what might be going on underneath. It's intended to hide the wounds that continue to be pushed down further and further the more you keep up your façade. There's usually a moment, though, when the mask gets chipped. Once this happens, some might try to glue it back together, but they discover that it will never again be the way it once was. Others might not want to fix it, instead discovering over time that the more chips break away, the more of who they really are is revealed. Each chip that breaks off can hurt, but it can also be freeing! You may not understand why the pieces fall the way they do, but at some point you discover that there is always a reason.

When you cover yourself up for so long, it can take years to chip away the mask. It's hard to be open to letting others in and difficult to start a journey of healing that will last the rest of your life. Others won't always understand. You may become protective of yourself after uncovering so much of your mask, leaving you feeling exposed and misunderstood. However, it's important to know that everyone wears a mask to some extent. For many, it's only a matter of time before they share their story. And when they do, remember that you don't have to fully understand their story to be by their side as they share what held them captive for so long.

I tell people that the story I share in this book is actually one of God's many stories of redemption in my life. It's a story about a broken human who covered herself with a mask, burying everything inside for years, until it was all too much to carry. My mask didn't slowly chip away. It completely shattered. I thought, *Now what?* as I stared at the broken pieces surrounding me.

I spent a lot of time searching for books that I hoped would help as I navigated heartbreak in all types of relationships, and as I am navigating singleness in my late thirties. I couldn't find anything. From the moment I discovered that I had been catfished, I heard God's voice clearly telling me, "*Stacey, you're going to write a book someday to help others in a similar situation feel less alone.*" This story is what I was searching for. It took seven years to get it to what you hold in your hands right now. I knew it would happen, but I didn't know the timing. I've learned through this process that my timing isn't God's timing!

This book is my story about being catfished and overcoming the trauma I endured, but it's also about what led up to that event . . . and what followed. It's about how I looked at all the shattered pieces of my mask and decided not to try to fix them, but instead to grow and continue to move forward toward where God was leading me. It's about my journey through heartbreak, building my relationship with Jesus, and finding healing and restoration for my whole body—emotionally, mentally, physically, and spiritually—and ultimately finding self-love along the way. This book is full of courageous vulnerability and true authenticity that I want you to see, notice, and unlock in yourself! *Unlocking Love* is a journey through my story that will also reveal more of yours, if you are open and willing to let it.

My Hope

I hope and pray that you will be able to connect, feel a little less alone, and allow yourself to pause and think about where you are on your own journey. You will read some of my journal entries as I processed through things. I encourage you to find a journal that speaks to you and allow yourself time at the end of each chapter to not only answer the Pause and Reflect questions but also to record anything that comes to mind or is on your heart. Through pausing and reflecting, I hope you discover an area in your life that you need to unlock, opening yourself up to revealing more about who God has created you to be! As you do so, my prayer for you is to be reminded that you are not alone.

I give to you my story. Enjoy the adventure that awaits you!

Stacey

Part 1

THE EVENT

June 27, 2016—Freedom Day

I WROTE THIS PRAYER in my journal before getting ready for the day:

> *I pray for forgiveness of my sins, my wrongdoings, my thoughts, and me trying to control my life. I pray that You, God continue to open my heart in prayer to You.*

A simple prayer of forgiveness.

A simple prayer to let go of controlling my life, which seemed to be spiraling out of control right before my eyes.

A prayer to open my heart back to Him.

The only plan I had for the day was to meet Laina, a friend I hadn't seen in a while. It was probably a thirty-minute drive to the restaurant, where I arrived early. I had told Dave earlier that morning that I was meeting a friend for lunch. So, after I parked, I looked at my phone before walking into the restaurant. I noticed I had a message from my internet friend Parker on Facebook Messenger. She wrote, "That is really f***ed up that you would write that to me!"

My heart started racing.

Anxiety crept in as I stood there, thinking to myself, *What is she talking about? What did I write that made her respond to me like that?* I scrolled up to reread the message she was referring to.

My heart sank.

My mind was like a cobweb that was about to be destroyed.

I immediately thought to myself, *I didn't write that! I have no recollection of writing that message!*

My next thought was, *Did my Facebook get hacked?*

I wrote a response back to Parker. Shortly afterward, Dave texted me, asking why I would have messaged that to her. I was like a drowning puppy desperately trying to paddle to the surface and defend myself. No matter what I was saying or telling either of them, they seemed to be infuriated.

You must be wondering what the message said. Dave and Parker had supposedly gone on a ski trip together, where Parker had broken her leg and had to be airlifted off the mountain. The last message that Facebook Messenger had me writing was, "Hi Parker! I hope you have a nice weekend on one good leg." Being the very empathic person I am, to have these words staring back at me gave me a sinking feeling that something was just. not. right.

Up walked Laina.

She saw the distress in my face, and as we hugged, she asked, "What's wrong?"

Shaking, I said, "Something weird is happening. I just don't know what to do, think, or say!"

We walked inside and grabbed a table as I began to explain what was going on. While I talked, my phone was blowing up with texts and Facebook messages, and I think that at one point Dave tried calling. This continued all through lunch. The one thing I remember is Laina looking me straight in the eyes, with major concern in hers, and saying, "Stacey, you have been talking to this guy for *how* long now and still haven't met? Something is so wrong with all of this! What are you going to do?"

The conversation between us went something like this . . .

Me: I don't know. All I know is that this feeling I have is literally making me sick. I know I didn't write that message! One of my friends, a few weeks ago, told me that she's ready to hire a private investigator to figure out who this person is. I told her not to. Not yet. I would set a date for Dave and me to meet, and it would need to happen.

Laina: Well, if this guy is real, he should be flying out here tomorrow to meet you! I think there's something you can do online to look up people who might not be who they say they are.

While Laina and I talked and ate—though my stomach was so upset I felt like throwing up—my phone was still blowing up. Multiple times I messaged Dave that I could not talk, but that didn't seem to matter. He persisted, and eventually even Sabrina began messaging me. (These names will make more sense going forward.)

After lunch, Laina gave me a hug and told me I needed to figure this out, and I knew she was right. This was the moment I found myself screaming inside my head, *Enough is enough!*

My mind was on overdrive on the way home. My phone was still dinging out of control with belittling texts and Facebook messages. I thought to myself, *Look at the timestamp.* The date was June 19, 2016, eight days earlier and around the time Dave and Parker had reportedly started their "off the grid" skiing trip.

I then looked on my Calendar App to see what day of the week June 19 had been. Father's Day Sunday. On that day I had driven an hour to meet my family for a late lunch. I looked at the time stamped on the message sent to Parker. Around 4:00 p.m. I then looked at the photo I had taken with my mom and dad before leaving the restaurant that day. It was stamped at around 3:30 p.m., which meant that I was driving home when the message was sent. Conclusion: I did *not* write that message! And I was far from crazy!

I prayed all the way back to the house, trying to wrap my head around what was going on and what I was going to do next. I stopped responding to Dave, Parker, Sabrina, or any other of the internet acquaintances associated with them, concerned that they might be trying to get into my head even more than they already had.

As I pulled into the garage, I remembered an MTV show that I used to watch in college: *Catfish: The TV Show.* If you are not familiar with the show, here's a quick synopsis. Nev, the host and executive producer, helps people who have an online dating relationship with someone they've never met in person. He investigates the emotional entanglement that ensues in order to uncover the truth. In most cases, the person being investigated is not who they have made themselves out to be.

According to Merriam-Webster Dictionary Online, the definition of *catfish* is, "a person who sets up a false personal profile on a social networking site for fraudulent or deceptive purposes."

I remember Nev taking photos of these people from their Facebook profiles and putting them into a search engine to discover if the person was who they said they were. I knew I needed to figure out how to do this!

I jumped out of my car, ran inside to my bedroom, closed the door, and put my laptop on my bed. I remember sitting there, legs criss-crossed, ready to figure this out! Thanks to YouTube, I found a clip about how to take a photo from Facebook and upload it into Google Image Search. This seemed easy enough.

I said a prayer as I went to Sabrina's profile. I dragged one of her photos into Google Image Search and hit *Enter*. What happened next is something I will always remember.

Staring back at me was a plethora of photos of "Sabrina." But the name on each of the photos was not Sabrina Caldwell. Instead, it was Stephanie Claire Smith, an Australian model who had a boyfriend named Josh and a best friend named Laura Henshaw.

I gasped. And I let out the biggest exhale I had experienced in the longest time.

In this moment, with just one image search, I felt the release of the load of bricks that had been holding me down and burying me more and more deeply!

Next up, I searched Kolbie Quinn. Up came Brooke Hogan, another Australian model.

Ashlee Phelps = Madi Edwards

Holly Noel = Helen Owen

Grace Carr = Gabrielle Epstein

Samantha Chelsey = Laura Henshaw (Stephanie Claire Smith's best friend)

Ellie = Sanne Alexandra (from Sweden)

Parker Shelton = Olivia Paladin

Hit after hit for these people I had spent the last year and a half talking to and sharing so much of my life, heart, and time with. I had been building "friendships" with all of them, only to discover that they were all fake. Furthermore, the photos of the real women and men with these names were being used to fabricate intricate lives not their own.

As I sat there in my new role as investigator, I was texting a friend and sharing what I found out because I knew I would need support to get through this. By 10:00 p.m. she was getting worried because I was no longer responding. The reason was that the last two people I needed to put into Google Image Search were Ari and Dave.

First, I put in some of Ari's photos. No hits, other than a photo found on some Asian site. Next, I put in some of Dave's photos. No hits.

Think, Stacey, think.

I remembered a few photos Dave had sent me of his house in California. I went back through my texts and screen shots and found them! I put the first one into a search and, *voila*! It was a house in La Jolla, California, overlooking the ocean. And who was staring back at me as the designer and owner of this home? David Caldwell.

However, his real name was Andrew Canter.

I sat there in awe as I took in everything. I started reading more about Andrew and the life he lived. His fiancé was Ariana, aka, Ari, the one name of all of them that hadn't changed. I went to Andrew Canter's Facebook page, along with Ari's, where I discovered a number of little things Dave had photoshopped out of the photos he had sent me, including Ari's engagement ring. There was another photo he sent me of himself (no head included, which should have been a red flag), which I put into a search. It came back as belonging to a model who had multiple tattoos. Dave had photoshopped these out of the photos he had sent me months earlier. Dave even took some of Andrew's story and made it all seem as though it were his life. Shocked doesn't begin to explain how I was feeling.

The question that surfaced now was, *Who the hell have I been talking to for the past almost seven years?*

chapter 2

What Shapes You?

GOD IS THERE through life's ups and downs, happiness and sadness, joys and hardships. He created these moments to remind us what the true meaning of life is: to enjoy the blessings that only He can give, no matter how hard life might be.

How do you start a puzzle? Do you sort all the pieces by color or isolate the border pieces? Do you start by putting together the outside frame, or do you assemble one section of the overall picture at a time?

We will never be able to clearly see the whole picture of our lives because only God has that ability. But as I look back on my nearly forty years on this earth, each puzzle piece of my life reminds me that there has been a reason for it.

Puzzle Section #1: My Childhood

I was raised in a loving, nuclear family consisting of my mom, dad, and younger brother. We lived in the country, went to mass every Sunday, camped during the summer months, and always had some type of

Labrador retriever, goldfish, or hermit crab as a pet. My parents were always there supporting me, watching me play basketball, try out for softball, and even attempt high jump one spring in high school. They had sat through many dance performances, piano recitals, academic accomplishments, awards, and so much more. They had always been present.

My parents raised my brother and me to be independent, well-rounded, caring individuals, protecting us from the evil in the world as much as they could. However, children are meant to explore, experience new things, make mistakes, and learn from them on our journey into adulthood.

I recalled the introduction of cordless phones; box computers; AOL Messenger; car phones that plugged into the cigarette lighter socket; Game Boy; cable TV; tanning beds; and, eventually, cell phones. Notice a pattern? All technology in some form or another.

I went from playing with baby dolls and playing school in my basement, creating mudpies in the sandbox, shooting hoops in my driveway, and sledding down the gigantic snow slide my dad had spent hours making every winter to talking to friends on my cordless phone in my bedroom and playing "SimCity" and "Oregon Trail" on our box computer downstairs. I was talking to people I didn't know on AOL Messenger and watching A *Wedding Story* and A *Baby Story* on TLC and music videos on MTV.

I started driving at sixteen, which is when my parents gave me my first cell phone, without a texting feature or internet. It was strictly for use in calling them when I arrived at my destination and then again when I was leaving, all to make sure I was safe. My innocence was left far behind as I grew up, but deep within I still dreamed of fairytale love from the books my mom had read to me and the Disney movies I had watched that featured a prince and princess.

Something important to know: I didn't date growing up. I had a solid group of girlfriends and was part of all different kinds of social groups. However, I did struggle to find my "fit"; as with so many others, my middle school years were the toughest. I had crushes in high school, asked a boy to our February Swirl dance and got turned down, and was shy around boys. I had no experience, had the fairytale mindset, and went out of my way to walk by a crush but didn't know what to say or how to hold a conversation. I longed to be liked by a boy, but no boy seemed interested or pursued me. I just didn't understand why.

I also faced shame from things I had explored and experienced as a child, which I didn't realize were part of normal development and curiosity. My child's mindset meant that I thought I was being punished for these things—that was why no boys were pursuing me. This kind of misperception can do a lot of damage to a child, and I have worked as an adult on healing in this area.

Puzzle Section #2: College

This shy girl got a scholarship to play basketball at a small private school thirty minutes from home in the "bigger" city. The specifics of my transformation in college could constitute another book!

I am the first to admit how naïve I was as I transitioned into college. Although the college I went to was Catholic, the student body was far from living a holy life. Being part of an athletic team my freshman year meant parties, late nights, and guys. I went to my first party, bonged my first beer, and began to experience life outside the safe bubble I had grown up in.

One night at a party I started talking to a guy from the basketball team who was a year older than me. It was fun, but I didn't know what to think about it all. We started talking more on AOL and found ourselves hanging out whenever we were at parties. I didn't know how to handle the situation because I was new to this feeling of possibly liking a guy who actually talked to me. I began to think of different imagined scenarios and to form fictional narratives in my mind rather than embracing the moment and going with the flow. We weren't even dating at this time, just talking! Nothing more came of our relationship other than our remaining friends.

Fast forward to the summer going into my sophomore year. I was taking a class at the community college, and one particular guy would strike up a conversation with me after every class. Later, I found out that he parked in the parking ramp just to walk out with me and talk—a ploy I had been oblivious to. He asked me out, and we started dating.

That summer was spent going to movies and to the beach, my first sober make-out sessions, and having my first "official" boyfriend.

As I started my sophomore year in college, I remember feeling as though he was moving too fast. I didn't know what to do about it because I had never been in a committed relationship before. One night when I was home visiting my parents, I remember telling my mom that I just wanted to experience dating. I broke up with this nice, caring guy before the school year began. This experience started my journey of becoming more comfortable talking to guys.

I stopped playing basketball after my sophomore year, stopped going home every weekend, and continued to hang out with my previous teammates. I met a group of girls who are still some of my close friends and enjoyed what college had to offer. This included going to bars, dancing with and grinding on complete strangers, making out on the dance floor, and walking home with my friends, heels in my hand because the cool pavement felt refreshing on my sore feet. Anyone else know what I'm talking about?

I went out on a few dates, but nothing serious transpired. My innocent inner child still felt as though I were being punished for things I had done. The only way I felt I could escape the guilt was to numb it by drinking and going out. I was holding onto the lie that no one would want a relationship with someone who already felt so broken. Not to mention that I was carrying a lot of Catholic guilt and shame.

With my college freedom came a lot of laughter, exploring, mistakes, and learning—beyond the academics. It wasn't until the final semester of my senior year that I decided to make a move that would change the trajectory of my life forever.

During the summer of 2008, I packed up my Chevy Malibu and moved to South Carolina to begin my teaching career and my next chapter in life. All by myself.

Puzzle Section #3: Post-College

Enter online dating.

At age 22 I logged onto Plenty of Fish, a free online dating site. I felt this was a way to put myself out there and get comfortable with dating, since I'd had only one boyfriend to that point. I began talking to one particular guy. I don't remember his name, but I do remember one of the photos he posted. Visualize a pool party with champagne spraying, surrounded by a lot of people. Totally not my type or scene, either then or now. But he seemed fun, so we began chatting on the site and eventually texting. He asked me to go to a Clemson game with him in the fall. I originally said yes, but after I had told a close friend about it, she put a little fear in me that I needed to hear.

She warned me about meeting a guy I'd never seen in person, in a place I'd never been, with people I had never met. I wanted to experience life and dating, not even thinking about my safety in this type of situation. How many times does this happen to women, especially innocent ones who are just looking to be and feel loved? Might this be you?

Before you say yes to a date, ask yourself:

- Do I feel safe?
- Will we be meeting in a public place?
- Have I told a trusted friend where I will be going?
- Who can I text or call if I feel my safety is at risk?

I ended up canceling going to the game, and the guy was not happy about it. At all. He made me feel guilty, telling me that he had already bought the tickets, which weren't cheap, and making me feel as though I had let him down. Even after canceling, he kept talking to me until I decided I wasn't mentally or emotionally in the best space to be dating anyone at that time.

I told him I thought it would be best for us to stop talking. If his previous reaction had been any indication, I knew he wasn't going to understand why I wanted to stop talking to him altogether. Needless to say, he didn't take this news well. Once again, he made me feel as though I deserved to be single (Red Flag #1).

During this time I got pretty good at making everything look fine on the outside . . . while feeling far from fine on the inside. I believe, in fact, that I started experiencing a mental breakdown. My world felt as though it were spinning out of control, and I was incredibly stressed trying to figure out how to balance everything in my life, all while trying to establish new friendships and teaching at a grade level I had never thought I would teach. I felt as though I couldn't cope or add anything new to my already overflowing plate. This just amplified my never feeling that I was enough.

I felt as if I were drowning while trying to be everything, do everything right, and make everyone happy! My mind and body felt out of control, and I didn't know where to go, what to think, whom to go to, or where to turn.

I was lost and exhausted.

Therapy, antidepressants, and endless nights of crying became part of my life. I chose to be cracked wide open as I began to uncover many years of unhealthy coping strategies. These included sweeping issues under the rug, making everything seem perfect on the outside, and controlling my food intake, which led me to struggle with anorexia, body dysmorphia, and becoming a compulsive exerciser. It was time to remove the mask I had been hiding behind for so many years. The layers were just starting to peel off, which left me feeling exposed.

The hardest person to find is yourself, but it's worth it! There is always hope!

I was driving to school one fall morning when I approached a curve I had driven many times. However, on that morning I remember thinking, *If I just kept going straight, would anyone truly miss me?*

Straight ahead was a big tree.

I chose to continue around the curve and made my way to school that morning, but I will never forget that moment.

In the darkest and lowest moments of our lives, we may find ourselves asking this question: *Will anyone truly miss me if I take my own life?* If that is you, know that you are not alone! According to the Centers for Disease Control (CDC), 12.3 million people in 2021 *thought* about taking their own lives!

As I look back, I realize that, if I hadn't taken that first step on the journey to expose myself and dig deeper, I wouldn't be where I am today. I'm here to tell you that it's not easy! The hardest person to find is yourself, but it's worth it! There is always *hope*!

While facing the anxiety and depression, I decided it was time to come home to the Mitten State. I would be closer to my family, friends, and support system, who would be just a couple of hours away rather than twelve.

Signs that you might be struggling mentally:

- Excessive worrying, fear, sadness
- Irritability or anger
- Avoiding family, friends, and social events
- Trouble sleeping
- Low energy
- Change in eating habits (increased hunger or lack of appetite)
- Alcohol or drug increase
- Feeling out of control
- Suicidal thoughts
- Changes in school or work performance

I hired a moving truck and packed up my final things, and the closest friend I had in South Carolina made the road trip back to Michigan with me. This friendship is one I will never forget. She showed the kind of love only a true friend could, even while I was at the lowest point in my life. She saw the struggles I endured, the exhaustion from my therapy sessions, the fear and hurt in my eyes, the darkness, and my lack of self-love. I know she also saw the hope, grace, and forgiveness I deserved and needed to grant myself in order to continue to heal, move forward, and find myself along the way.

Knowing she would now be twelve hours away was challenging for me. She was the person I turned to, the person who accepted and loved me for who I was even in this tough season I was going through. She saw me when I wasn't able to see myself. She was always there for me, but though I told her I didn't want anything to change, deep down

I knew it would. A long-distance relationship of any type, whether friendship or romance, is challenging to maintain when the two of you are not living through everyday things together. I know this friend will be reading these words someday, and I want to thank her.

So, dear friend, thank you for being there for me when I needed it most. You will always be part of my life and an integral part of my story, my puzzle.

Think about what has shaped your own life puzzle.

- What puzzle pieces are already in place?
- Which pieces are still waiting to be put into the frame of your life?
- Which ones are lost and need to be found to become part of the picture?
- What puzzle sections are you holding onto and might need to release?
- Are there areas in your life in which you might not feel you are enough?

I encourage you to release whatever you're holding on to and thank God for each piece of your life that He has intricately put into place.

chapter 3

Going Fishing

WE ALL KNOW what a catfish looks like. It's a fish that looks like a cat, whiskers and all, that is caught in large rivers, streams, and inland lakes. In 2012 I began watching an MTV show called *Catfish: The TV Show*. Little did I know that, three years earlier, I had begun living my own *Catfish* episode that would last for almost seven years.

The Bait

One fall night in 2010, I was sitting at a high-top table in a bar my friend and I often went to. I remember my phone dinging, signaling that I had received a text. I flipped open my phone—yes, I had an actual flip phone—to read the text. Do you recall the guy I had talked to online when living in South Carolina? It was him! I was shocked because it had been a good year since I had basically said, "Peace out!" I never expected to hear from him again, especially since he had told me he was living the "California lifestyle."

We started chatting a bit here and there as I continued online dating. Although dating was nothing super serious for me at that time, he always made me feel as though no one else would be good enough for me and that we just needed to meet and try things out. However, whenever I asked him when he'd like to meet, there was always a reason not to (Red Flag #2).

At this stage he told me he was building his company and traveling to different countries quite a bit. I never thought much of it because I was living my own life, establishing my career, continuing my therapy work, and going out on weekends. I remember a time he mentioned flying to Michigan and taking me to a Tigers game. I thought, *Great! Let's do it! We'll finally meet and see what this is.* Well, that plan was short lived; he told me he was stuck in Turkey for business. My gut reaction was that this seemed a little odd, but, looking back now, I realize that this was the point at which his smooth talking began. (As you read on, pay attention to how often I mention my gut. There is a reason!)

It's impossible to put almost seven years of manipulation, gaslighting, narcissism, and possibly dealing with a psychopath into a neat paragraph. There is nothing nice to say when describing a person who does this to another. Keep in mind that all of this built up over time. There were so many moments when I remember coming home from a date or even dating for an extended period, only to be pulled back into Dave's emotional and mental grasp. (I knew him only as Dave, the name he had given me.)

The morning after I lost my virginity, at the age of 27, I remember calling him on my way home and hearing him tell me how disappointing and disgusting I was for having sex for the first time the way I did. This was the first time I remember him shaming me. I didn't know what to say or do, but I knew how he affected me. I was already beating myself up and didn't need someone I hadn't even met making me feel even more dirty, guilty, and shameful.

The Cast

In 2014, after breaking things off with someone I had been dating, I expressed to Dave that my emotions were all over the place about him. I didn't know what was going on between us, if anything at all. Someone who will play a significant role in all of this was Dave's best friend, Ari. I had known about Ari for quite some time. He told me they were best friends and lived together (Red Flag #3), but as time went on he shared that they had dated and were still trying to figure out what their relationship entailed. Yet he always reassured me that there was something special about me and that he wanted to see how true our connection was. He told me not to lose hope and to trust him! (Red Flag #4: Don't trust anyone you have never met!) It was around this time that I decided I would fully commit to not dating anyone else until Dave and I met, and he was aware of this decision.

I lived in a fairytale mindset—not surprising, considering my history growing up and with dating, not to mention that I was still in a vulnerable state of healing. I asked Dave, "What do you even see in me? I'm like this little peasant girl, like Cinderella, and you are the prince. What is it that makes you want to continue to talk to me?"

Little did I know then how messed up things were about to get.

One night as Dave and I were talking, he asked if there was a job or career I might want other than teaching. I explained that my dream since I was five years old had been to be a teacher, and I had never thought about doing anything else. However, the reality was that I was burnt out. He then suggested, "Well, think about what else you might want to do, and I'll make it happen."

Wasn't that just so "prince-like"? The successful businessman, living in California and traveling the world, offers to rescue the meek little peasant girl struggling to live off a teacher's salary and rethinking what she wants to do with her life, where she wants to be, and who she wants to be with. I honestly thought the situation was ridiculous, but it got me thinking, *Is there something else out there I could see myself doing*?

I began researching what else I might be interested in and kept coming back to event planning. I was organized and enjoyed making people happy, and fun events always seemed to bring joy to others. I started looking for event planning positions in the area, but, unfortunately, the pay and the hours, along with what looked like quite a workload, didn't seem to fit my lifestyle. When I mentioned this to Dave, he told me he had a friend who was a successful event planner. He then told me that his friend was starting her own event planning business and that he would tell her about me.

Enter Laurel.

Dave told me more about Laurel and asked me to get a résumé together to send her. I thought, *How do I write a résumé with only a teacher's background?* Dave encouraged me to think about the skills I had as an educator and how I could apply them to event planning. Keeping this in mind, I came up with an impressive résumé to send to Laurel. Once I did, I emailed it to her and waited.

Laurel was hoping to have her event planning business up and running within a year. She made sure to be up front with me and asked if, with my lack of experience, I would be willing to put in the hours and everything else I would need to make this work. Laurel didn't know that I am one of the hardest workers and that, when I commit, I commit one hundred percent!

Dave asked me how I felt about moving to California, where the new job would be. My gut reaction was that I didn't want to, but I knew that, to get out of teaching, I would have to make this drastic move. This also meant that Dave and I could try things out to see if there was a more serious connection between us. He made me think and feel as though there were something there emotionally, mentally, and physically.

While I waited on the new job, Dave and I continued to talk on the phone for hours. On March 14, 2015, I remember getting off the phone and feeling frustrated and upset with him. I had brought up wanting to come to California for my spring break to check everything out and spend time with him. However, he said he would be in Dubai. I remember shutting down and not saying much after this news. I was frustrated with what seemed to be his lack of understanding about how big a move this would be for me.

This was the night I began writing about what was going on in my journal, trying to process what I was thinking and how I was feeling. This entry was written in a letter form to Dave:

Dear Dave,

I dislike going to bed upset or without having an issue or problem discussed. This is one thing I want in my marriage, to never go to bed without at least trying to resolve and talk out an issue because you never know what will happen during the night, morning, or next day (Ephesians 4:26).

I need time to process how I'm feeling in my head and heart before I express it. I will always be open and honest with you, but sometimes it takes time. I grew up holding a lot in. It took years of therapy for me to be comfortable and willing to openly express my feelings as they surface. With you, it's different because a conversation I would want to have face to-face is not feasible right now. According to research done by Albert Mehrabian, 55 percent of communication is nonverbal, and 38 percent is based on tone. Texting provides neither. I'm frustrated, you're irritated, and I feel like it's a never-ending cycle between us!

Why am I frustrated? I am frustrated because I just don't feel that you completely understand what a life-altering time this is for me. I am unsure of everything in my life right now. Will this move even take place? What will it be like when I'm living there? I'm feeling scared, excited, and unsure. As you know, I'm a planner. I'm trying hard to go with the flow of things and to wholeheartedly trust that everything will work out as it is meant to. However, I have a job right now that is making more cuts. I have coworkers and a principal planning for next year's staffing. Am I just getting my hopes up for nothing? When I put my mind on something, I give one hundred percent to make it happen. I know a business takes time to build, but knowing that Laurel is thinking her business will start the first week of July now makes me anxious.

I question whether this is even going to happen. I need you to at least try to understand what is happening in my life. What will be happening soon is not easy for me, which is why I thought spring break would be the perfect time for me to come out to California to check everything out and spend time with you. Yes, I know you have to go to Dubai, but I just want you to be back by then.

The one time I have a whole week off and want to spend it with you, in an area that I might end up living in, you won't even make an attempt to be there? I feel frustrated when I know you're choosing to be in Dubai instead of wanting to meet me. I know you have business to keep up with, and, although Michigan doesn't hold any work-related business, it does hold *me*! I don't feel you understand that it hurts me when you fly all around the country and world to do business and visit friends, but you never make an effort to come here. Sometimes I feel like you tell me one thing or something you will do, but it either changes or you don't end up following through or you just put it off longer, which in my eyes is showing and telling me that you're putting me off . . . again.

I find myself wondering: What if I told you we either meet by this date, or else? The "or else" kills me because I don't ever want an "or else." I don't want to be the one to issue an ultimatum, or vice versa. I could never see myself without you in my life. If you don't know it by now, I'm different from other girls you've come across. I am who I am, and I will not change for anyone. You have my heart—you always have—and I've never been more afraid of it getting broken. I want to be set apart from others, and sometimes I feel like I'm part of the "competition" to win you over, which I can't stand! Just as any woman, I want a man to pursue me.

I have bawled my eyes out for the past hour. I looked in the mirror before starting to write this and, through red, blood-shot eyes, I asked, "Stacey, why are you crying over a man you've never met?" The answer: Because, however crazy it might seem, I care about you.

I hope this helps in expressing my feelings and helps you to become less irritated because I *do* love you!

Stacey

I'm giving you permission right now to pause and take that in. There may be questions tumbling through your mind. Maybe even *How many red flags did it take for you to see what this guy was doing to you, Stacey?* My response to you and to myself is that he had my mind wired to make me think and feel the way he wanted me to, and always to retreat back to him. I was always seeking his approval, even while he was making me feel like I was second, third, or fourth best. Then, in his narcissistic way, he was pulling me back and making me feel like I would eventually be the one who mattered most. That none of the other women, the trips, or his lack of seeing me really mattered.

Again, he used my fairytale mindset to dig even more deeply into my psyche. This made me share with him more and more openly and honestly about my heart's desires and what I thought I wanted in an ideal boyfriend at that time. I became entangled in the fairytale of it all and didn't know the extent of his villainous ways.

May 2015 through June 2016 brought a lot of processing, which I did through journaling. The following entries supply some of the missing pieces of the puzzle that I didn't see then but recognized when rereading my journals to write this book.

The Hook

May 2, 2015

. . . As of last night, Dave told me that Laurel would not be starting the event planning this year. Although I was disappointed, I feel as though God has another plan for me. I'll be sending my résumé to Dave's company sometime this week. I pray and hope something is available for me in the next couple of months. Through this process, I continue to learn more about myself.

- » I have started to try to let things be.
- » I don't have control over what might happen in the future.
- » I'm trying to be more spontaneous, reminding myself that life is too short to be unhappy and not live it fully.

I never thought I would end up not wanting to teach. I don't know what the future might hold, but I do know I'm ready for the change and adventure ahead. I pray that God blesses me with both. I pray that He will show me where He wants me and what He wants me to do.

June 30, 2015

At this moment I am by a stream in the park. Quite fitting, since in the past few weeks there has been a constant stream of emotion flowing through me. I don't even know when the last day was that I haven't cried. What has caused a lot of it is a love that is so deep and crazy that I can't help but cry. I'm in love with a man who lives 2,298 miles away. A man I have never met, whom I talk to daily, and whom I'd like to be with every single day. He's not like any man I've met before and one I'm afraid I'll never meet. (Oh, the irony of this statement!)

> He's a man I have such a deep connection with, and he knows more about me than many others do. He calms me down, tells me to trust in him, to relax, and to be confident in what we have. He has my whole heart, and I'm scared to death of it being broken. He constantly puts up with my emotions, my doubts, and my worries about him, us, and teaching—and who loves me nonetheless. He's the only one I have let my guard down with. I honestly don't know if I could ever feel like I do about him with someone else. What do I have to worry about, then?
>
> » His not waiting for me and falling for someone else.
> » His losing feelings for me.
> » His realizing I'm too emotional to handle.
> » His giving up on me.
> » My failing him.
> » My lack of confidence that someone like him could love me.
> » My feeling that no one else will ever measure up to him.
>
> He continues to reassure me of the connection he feels with me, and he has recently expressed that he is in love with me.
>
> As I sit here, listening to the stream, I have my own tears flowing down my cheeks not knowing what to do. There is literally a pit in my stomach that I cannot shake (Red Flag #5). How do I get through this next year before moving my whole life when I'm feeling like this?

During the summer of 2015, I needed to figure out where to live for a year. I didn't want to pay unreasonable amounts of money, so one of my former principals told me her sister was looking for someone to rent out one of her bedrooms. It seemed as though this would be the perfect set-up for the year I had ahead of me. It was five minutes from school, I'd save money, and it would be a win-win for both me and the family! I was incredibly grateful for her sister's hospitality and for allowing me into her life. During this year I did my own thing and was in and out, keeping myself busy. But so much happened emotionally, mentally, and even physically that no one will ever understand, nor will I be able to express the abuse, which I can now name as such, that I endured from Dave. None of this was okay!

The Drag

Fast forward to the fall 2015. I was fully committed to Dave and found myself writing him lengthy, very vulnerable emails and spending hours on the phone at night talking about everything under the sun. There were many days I went to school on only three hours of sleep. (Remember, he told me he lived in California, which was three hours behind me.) He "introduced" me to some of his other girlfriends, who I started chatting with on Facebook Messenger. I had not written in my journal for months, until I was up north at my parents' house, when I wrote the following:

> *October* 18, 2015
>
> As I woke up this morning and saw the sunrise over the lake, I thought of how beautiful this day will be. I love fall! Beautiful trees, chilly mornings and nights, trips to the apple orchard, running outside, and just enjoying the beauty God has created for us to enjoy.
>
> This might be my last fall in Michigan, which makes me want to take it all in. The upcoming months are about to hold a lot of change. I know my mom is very worried about my move. She wants me to be safe, and I know she wants me to be in close proximity. However, I feel like she doesn't understand the urge I have for a change, my eagerness to try something new and be adventurous. My friends have been supportive, and I need to continue to remember that this is what I want.
>
> This past week there have been some high and low points.
>
> » Going to the Red Wings game with a friend.
> » Realizing I need my anxiety meds and that's okay.
> » Spending time with my mom.
> » Talking with Dave two nights this week; first for four hours and the second time for two hours. (I wasn't joking when I mentioned before that we talked on the phone for hours at a time!)
>
> Our conversations are never ending, and there are really no lulls in them. The first night we talked about my move, about Ari, about

> our definition of "home" in relation to our parents, about where we would want to settle, and about his properties (three in LA and one each in Texas, Miami, New York, and Dubai). (Red Flag #6: If someone has multiple properties all over the country and different parts of the world, ask more questions, dig a little deeper, and be on guard.)
>
> The second night we talked about sexual things. There were words he shared with me that I had never heard before. We also talked about our differing views of sex. Dave mentioned that, if I were to have sex with someone else, I'd better tell him. I did ask him how he would feel if this ended up happening. He told me he really didn't know but that he did know we would have to have a talk. He told me he knew that, when I had sex, I would be looking for that emotional connection rather than it just "being" sex, which he expressed as being the way he views it. For me, he is the next and last person I want to be with on all levels, and I will do everything to show him this.

I'm giving you permission, again, to stop and ask, "What the . . . (you fill in the blank)?" Yes, I know. Just keep reading.

One day Sabrina, Dave's cousin turned sister (don't ask), asked me how I knew I loved Dave. I became emotional because I took this question very seriously. I never had thought about how I knew until she asked me. This is what I wrote to her on Facebook Messenger:

> How do I know I love, and am in love with, Dave?
>
> I know that I am in love with him because your asking how I know brings tears to my eyes. The emotions I feel in my soul flip, rise, and surface. I have never before known what love has felt like, and I've never been in love with anyone the way I am with Dave.
>
> How do I know?
>
> I just do. It's just a feeling I can't describe. It's a feeling that is scary, especially under the circumstances that he and I are in.
>
> How do I know?
>
> Because I don't see myself with anyone else. I have not kissed or done anything with a guy since February, and I don't want to. The thought of being with someone else before meeting and seeing what Dave and I might have makes my stomach turn. I could really care

less about what he does for a living, who he knows, or how much money he has. He knows me for me. All my flaws, doubts, and worries, and he still is there for me and loves me.

I think part of me has tried, a few different times, to push him away because of where I come from and how different we are. In my eyes, I felt like he is way too good for me and could do so much better. Even though I have hurt him, annoyed him, and irritated him, and in his words "I blew him off" when I could have met him almost seven years ago for the Clemson game, he still hasn't given up on me. Through it all, he has continued to talk to me and message me, and the love has just developed over time.

How do I know?

When he showed me part of his emotional side this year, it broke me open. It was the thing I'd been waiting to hear from him in order for me to feel "special" to him. Also, him surprising me by sending me flowers at school was something I had dreamed about but never thought would happen. Yes, I have told you there is still a part of that once very tall wall of mine that needs to be broken down, but that part is a tiny piece that is waiting to be in his presence. I so long to be able to touch, hold, and hug him and for him to do the same to me.

How do I know?

Because I'm an incredibly strong (too strong sometimes) woman, and he sees right through that. He knows that, although I am strong, I am also sensitive and emotional. I wear my heart on my sleeve. I feel like I can tell him anything—which might annoy him, but we are able to talk about it, and everything ends up being fine.

How do I know?

The communication we have is on a deep emotional level, since that's all we have. I just thought today when I was driving, *He must really love me because who else would talk on the phone with someone for hours and have nonstop conversations*? Neither of us likes talking on the phone very much at all, except with each other. He has my heart. He's had it for a couple of years now, but I've been too stubborn to admit it.

I was trying to find a guy closer to where I live, knowing in my heart that nothing would ever come of any other relationship until

> Dave and I met. I feel like no one understands, and, honestly, no one else has to because it's our love story. I've always told myself I'd never wait around for a guy, but this is exactly what I find myself doing. However, it feels different. He has always been the "What if?" guy.
>
> How do I know I not only love Dave but am in love with him? The feeling I have in my heart and soul. Period.

Somewhere in cyberspace are all the conversations and responses Sabrina wrote to me during that year. As I look back now, I keep on thinking, *Who was it that was responding to all of my messages?*

I cannot put into words what happened between that last entry, written in October 2015, and May 2016. In my journal, I included simple sentences of thanksgiving and little affirmations for the day in order to stay positive. I remember starting to write these because one of Dave's friends suggested that I write something positive each day since I sounded like I was depressed or in a funk. (Hmm, I wonder why?) Let me try to recap this time for you, as I was trying to hold it all together.

I was being pulled in every direction imaginable.

» I was giving it my all as a teacher because, no matter what, my students have always meant the world to me. No matter what I was going through personally or trying to figure out in my own life, they were always in the forefront of my mind.

» I was trying to balance continuing a relationship with this person I had never met but felt the strongest connection to emotionally and mentally, while knowing in my gut that something felt off. He was telling me it was my overthinking mind on overdrive that fed me these thoughts (Red Flag #7).

» I was trying to convince my family and friends that I was okay and that the planned move was exactly what I wanted. Yet inside I was literally dying, unsure of who I was any longer, what to do, or what to say, while trying to defend this "relationship" while being exhausted beyond belief.

I felt sick doing things for and sending videos to Dave that made me feel dirty. He critiqued different things and sent me uncomfortable videos to watch. None of this felt right. . . and never seemed good enough for him. Everything in me was screaming *Help!* But I never could admit this to myself or others. I wasn't ready to do so.

The manipulation and emotional, mental, and physical abuse were unraveling me at a speed I couldn't comprehend or process. I pulled away from my family and friends and basically hid. I didn't want to go out because I didn't want to update my friends and say out loud what I knew felt crazy. I had Dave, Sabrina, and others telling me daily to just relax and stop worrying and overthinking so much!

According to Verywellhealth.com, "Manipulative behavior refers to a person's use of gaslighting, love bombing, and other styles of interaction in a relationship used to gain power or influence over another. These tactics often include attempts to damage another person's emotional and mental well-being."

Signs of manipulation include:

» Twisting the facts
» Bullying
» Lying
» No accountability
» Criticizing
» Giving the silent treatment
» Causing doubt, confusion, and uncertainty

If you are feeling something similar to any or all of this, know that you are not crazy! You are not overthinking! You are not worrying for nothing! What you are feeling and thinking is real. It is your intuition telling you that something is not right. I will be the first to say that, until you are ready to admit it, it might feel as though you are in a crazy tailspin. You are about to read that it was still another month and a half before I was ready to face the facts and listen to myself. If this is you—if you don't feel ready to admit it yet but have a gut feeling that something isn't right—please, just pause. Write it out. Call a friend. Message me! More than anything else, know *that you are not alone!*

At this point you might be wondering, *Why didn't you ever Facetime or Skype?* Dave had plenty of reasons not to. He told me he had been a Navy Seal and that the amount of information someone could get from the little camera in their computer was unreal. What did I do? I questioned him multiple times, but he always seemed to have just the right words that got me hooked even further. The emotional and mental connection was deep, and when something gets into you that deeply, it becomes that much more challenging to listen to *yourself*. Instead, you listen to the other person, the one who is feeding you the misinformation. This is manipulation.

According to Healthline.com, "Gaslighting is a form of emotional abuse and manipulation. Gaslighting happens when an abuser or bully makes you question your beliefs and perception of reality." Here are some signs Healthline.com gives regarding gaslighting and what you might feel when being gaslit.

The person:

» Insists you said or did things you know you didn't do.
» Denies or scoffs at your recollection of events.
» Calls you "too sensitive" or "crazy"' when you express your needs or concerns.

You:

» Believe you can't do anything right.
» Have an urge to apologize all the time.
» Have frequent feelings of nervousness, anxiety, or worry.
» Have a persistent sense that something isn't right, though you can't identify exactly what's wrong.

During this time I was getting to know all of Dave's friends on Facebook Messenger, which in itself was far from healthy. There were many situations when I said something that to me was totally normal but that was taken way out of context and resulted in a huge ordeal.

I always felt as though I were in the wrong. Then Dave always asked about it. I'd try to explain what had happened, which led to his feeding me statements that made me feel that I had done or said something wrong. Just reading that sentence might make your head spin—which mine was doing constantly. Somehow, I was viewed as the crazy one. This is what is referred to as gaslighting.

I also felt self-conscious and pressured to look better, be healthier, and be sexier. For someone who had struggled with anorexia and body dysmorphia in the past, this brought to the surface all my insecurities. I wasn't sleeping well, never had a regular menstrual cycle, worked out to escape, and cut my hair short and dyed it a deep brown, which made it look black. To be honest, my hair matched what I was feeling on the inside: dark, lost, hopeless, and in a black hole.

Everyone was telling me about Dave, whether I wanted to hear it or not. And all of these conversations happened over Facebook Messenger (Red Flag #8). Even when I tried to get off Facebook, there was no way I could just keep Facebook Messenger. Sabrina made up some story about why she and I couldn't chat via text. I continued to write and send Dave in-depth emails, which ended up fueling what he would say to me, making me continuously feel as though I were in a crazy cycle.

I clearly remember staying up one night into the early hours of the morning talking to him. The next day he mentioned our having talked about his dad, who supposedly had passed away years earlier. I told him that I didn't remember him saying anything about his dad the night before. He became so defensive. I remember the conversation going something like this:

> "Do you even listen to what I tell you? That was a really deep emotional part of me that I shared with you, and you don't even remember!"
>
> "I appreciate your sharing such an emotional part of your relationship about your dad with me. I was listening to you the whole night, and that would be something I would definitely remember."
>
> "But you don't! You must have fallen asleep while talking to me. I'm pretty sure you have done that before when talking to me."

"Dave, I do my very best to be as alert as possible when we talk because I know how rare it is. It's a special time that I get with you, and I cherish it."

"Well, I guess what I told you about my dad wasn't that special if you fell asleep and don't remember it."

"I didn't fall asleep!" (I then found myself asking, *Did I fall asleep? It was probably like two in the morning, and I probably was tired. Could I have possibly dozed off?* No!)

I have always remembered this argument. I remember feeling that something about it was off. It wasn't until later that I learned that this incident is a prime example of what it means to be gaslighted.

PAUSE AND REFLECT

Have you felt or experienced any of the following?

Are you experiencing them now?

- Your gut telling you that something doesn't feel right, but you continue to push it aside.
- Empty promises to meet up.
- The person claiming to have multiple homes around the world.
- Modes of communication being stifled.
- No Facetime or video calls.
- Oversharing, even when it feels uncomfortable.
- Overexplaining yourself.
- Second guessing what you said.
- Irrational thoughts or feelings.
- Making excuses or trying to defend the other person or the relationship in an unhealthy way.
- Feeling always in the wrong.
- Feeling yourself to be in a never-ending cycle.
- Depression.
- Family and friends expressing their worry.
- Pulling away from family and friends.
- Sleepless nights.
- Changes in menstrual cycle.
- Outside appearance slowly or drastically changing.

If this list is bringing to the surface emotions in you, I encourage you to pause and think about the reason behind these emotions and who you can trust to share what's been going on.

chapter 4

The Fish Is Set Free

The Surrender

May 8, 2016 (Mother's Day)

I just spent the last day and a half with my beautiful mother! We had such a wonderful time, and I miss her already. When she left for home, I cried because it had all gone too fast. I've been trying to enjoy the time and moments with her, my family, and my friends. These are memories I will cherish forever. I also feel that I will end up disappointing her or letting her down in some way with my wanting to move.

I'm so unsure of my future. I have so much on my heart and mind that I feel that no one understands, nor do I fully know how to express it all without it sounding crazy, irrational, or as if I'm over-reacting. All of which I seemed to be doing when talking to Dave the other night. I tried to express my feelings, but none of it came out clearly, and none of it makes sense in my own mind, so how would he even try to understand it?

He's not the one sitting alone every night. He's not the one who has been without the opposite sex and touch in any way, shape, or form. He's actually with other girls trying to "figure things out" with them. He's not the one picking up his whole life, leaving a career he thought he'd be in for forever, and moving across the United States. He doesn't get it, nor do I expect him to, but I would like him to try to see and feel or understand what I'm going through!

Sabrina told me that he wasn't "too thrilled" about my reacting the way I did when he called the other night. Well, I wanted to respond with the fact that I wasn't "too thrilled" he didn't even attempt to call me or think about leaving a voicemail or assume I was "out" at 9:30 at night! I'm not "too thrilled" he hasn't tried talking to me a little more or asking me how my time with my mom had been! I'm not "too thrilled" he hates it when I become overly emotional. I'm not "too thrilled" he doesn't send me flowers, write me an email, answer some of my questions, or make me feel a little more special. Yes, talking on the phone is our special time, but sometimes I need more!

Let's start with actually meeting! Show some type of emotion, feelings, excitement! Stop *telling* me and start *acting*! I'm not "too thrilled" he told me, "Well, maybe we shouldn't talk as much when I'm (he's) home (in South Carolina)." Seriously?! Yes, that'll solve all the problems! I'm not "too thrilled" with this whole situation and feeling like he is the one making out like a bandit.

No, I don't know his feelings on everything or everyone he's trying to figure things out with, but I'd like to try to understand. Everyone seems to be nice, good, genuine, beautiful people. How can I not overthink? How can I not fully trust him? He's screwing, vacationing with, and "dating" all these other girls, but I'm the one he has the deep conversations with for hours on the phone!

Maybe I am angry. I'm angry that he doesn't seem to want to think or try to understand my point of view. I'm tired of apologizing for expressing my feelings and him not being "too thrilled" about my doing so. He wants me to openly tell him things but then has no clue, for days afterward, what to say in response.

None of this is fun for me! He's having the time of his life while trying to figure all of this out, and here I am, just waiting around!

Why can't I just say, "Eff it! I deserve to be treated better than this!" and let it go? I want to be treated right and cared for, and above all to feel loved! I come back to: Actions speak louder than words. I've invested so much of my time, energy, thoughts, tears, and love into this relationship. It's time for him to show me, and he has until the week of June 20 to do so. What scares me the most, though, is that I know he won't.

> *Prayer:*
> *Please Lord God, I pray for peace in my heart, mind, and soul. I pray that You will remind me daily to cherish the moments right now—not a month, six months, or a year from now. I pray for the peace to know You have my plan in Your hands. I pray that You will put Your hand on my shoulder to remind me of Your love and peace. I pray that You will take all of the heaviness and uncertainty when my thoughts and anxiety get the best of me. I pray for Your forgiveness in my wrongdoings, thoughts, and anxiousness. There's nothing I want more right now, in this moment, than the peace that everything is going to be okay. That everything will work out. Thank You for loving me for the woman I am. I love You, Lord, forever and ever. Amen.*

This was my moment of ultimate surrender. Fifty days later my life would again change forever!

The Splashing

I was spiraling. Splashing around like a fish being dragged through the water and eager to be set free. For the next month I continued to write prayers for guidance and peace and for God to lead me to where He saw me being. The unraveling was beginning, and, as Gabrielle Stone mentions in her bestselling book *Eat, Pray, #FML*, when a sweater has a piece of yarn hanging from it, we have the tendency to pull it. The more we pull on it, the more we come to realize that it always leads to an end. The splashing was getting out of control, and the things I was being told by Dave, Sabrina, and others were unimaginable.

It was twelve days before Dave and I were finally scheduled to meet when I was told by one of the girls he was "figuring things out with" that she was pregnant by him. I also had just found out that my teaching placement for the following year was to be at another school and for another grade level! My feelings were all over the place, and I felt numb and jumbled up inside. Throughout all this turmoil, I was asking two questions:

1. What does God have planned for me?
2. What is to be my next step in my journey of life?

From June 9 through June 24, I wrote a prayer prompt each day:

- God is the most powerful, and He will protect me.
- Keep God at the center of my life.
- God is good. He forgives, is full of grace, and loves me unconditionally.
- God is washing away my sin; therefore, I do not have to fear or feel ashamed of what I've done.
- Cry out to God and trust in His plans for my life.
- I am worthy of God's plan for my life of happiness, love, and being loved.
- Hope in His provision for my life.

June 24, 2016

I am writing to hopefully help express my feelings and just get them out of my mind! Sabrina and I have talked, and she is sharing more intimate details about when she and Dave are together. It's messed up! It's not easy to hear, but I want my friends to be able to talk to and share anything with me. There is a part of me that is feeling so apprehensive. I can only pray and hope I don't get hurt or screwed over in the end!

Sabrina has made comments today that leave me wanting to shout, "*What the hell is going on?! Is this all some kind of an imaginary fantasy I'm living in?*" Whenever I feel that I'm in a good place, doubt, uncertainty, and uneasiness all creep in. No one gets it! No one understands! I care so much about others and want others to be happy, but at what cost? When will it be my turn? I just wish someone could relate. I just wish someone would listen and not think I'm crazy!

Even if they don't say it out loud, I know what's going through my family and friends' minds because it's going through mine! I must remind myself in times like these to put my trust in God. He's the only One who knows what is to come for me. I'm excited, but also so scared. A big part of me just wants to make the leap of faith and the huge jump forward, not knowing where I will land. However, there's the innocent, apprehensive, planner side of me that is thinking,

No matter how bumpy life gets along the way, God will not lead me astray!

Be safe!

Is this safe?

What are you doing?

Why do you let him and others treat you like this?

Why are you still waiting around?

Do you really know for sure if Dave and these friends are legit?

There are so many red flags, Stacey, so why are you "sticking it out"?

Because I believe! I believe in true love. I believe and trust in God and His steering me in the right direction. I believe in myself that I need to follow my heart for once, take the risks that might come along the way. I believe I can and will do this! Who knows what will happen? But I trust God. No matter how bumpy life gets along the way, God will not lead me astray!

"The LORD is my Shepherd . . ." (Psalm 23:1).

Let me tell you, this sheep was not just wandering aimlessly any longer. She was completely lost and needed to be saved! The Lord did just that only three days later.

Now I pick up where I left off in chapter 1; feel free to reread it if you'd like. The splashing was about to stop, Dave would end up being caught, and I would finally be unhooked and set free!

By this time my friend was blowing up my phone, and I asked her if I could just come over. Rushing over there with my laptop in hand, I tried to explain everything I had just discovered. I was telling her things when the puzzle pieces started snapping into place. Such as Dave telling me a week or so earlier that his sister was in the hospital having her baby, who was born on June 21 and named Lincoln Michael. Through my stealthy investigating, I found out that Ari's sister has a little boy named Lincoln! As I was sharing everything, I was trying to wrap my head around the whole situation and what my next steps might be. My friend suggested, "I have a cousin who is a detective. Maybe I could reach out to see if there is anything we can do to figure out who this person might be and if there is any way to find him or press charges." This is exactly what we did.

Her cousin told me there wasn't any way to track via Facebook or the emails I had written to Dave. However, there was one thing I could try in order to figure out his actual location. I would be sent a link, which I would then send on to Dave. It would end up being a dead link, but it would pinpoint Dave's cell location and where he was at that exact moment. At this point I was willing to try anything, even though I was scared that Dave would know something was up, since I had already been short and a lot quieter than usual with him all night.

I left my friend's and drove back to the house. However crazy it might sound, I don't remember crying throughout this whole night! Instead, my mind, body, and soul were riding high on adrenaline. I actually felt a sense of lightening that I will never be able to put into words.

Once back in my bedroom, I sat on the floor between the side of the bed and the wall. I had been texting Dave a little bit here and there, asking whether he had time to chat. He, of course, did not, but I told him I needed to know what was going on. Not surprisingly, he claimed that he didn't know what I was talking about. I played it cool and tried to keep it that way.

So, there I was playing detective. My friend sent me the dead link, and I found myself trying to figure out how I could send it to Dave without his becoming suspicious and wondering why I was sending him a link that didn't work. What did Detective Stacey do? I found another link and randomly sent it to see if I could throw him off. He told me it was to a particular website. *Okay, good! It worked*, I thought.

Have I mentioned that at this point I thought I was going to shit my pants? I didn't have a clue who I was really dealing with, and fear was beginning to creep in. I copied the link to the text box and hit *Send*. Then I sat there in anticipation, waiting. What seemed like forever was actually only a minute or so, when he responded with, "That link didn't take me anywhere, but it gave me a message saying it wasn't an active link."

Phew! It worked, I thought as I responded to him and said how weird it was that it wasn't working! I texted my friend, telling her that he had just responded. Minutes later I received a text back: "Are you sure you want to know where he is located?"

"No, I'm not sure—but yes, I need to know."

Screenshot sent.

Oh. My. Gosh! This is the point where I believe the floodgates opened wide, as I sat there with the location points of this person staring back at me.

Anderson, South Carolina.

The town and state where the guy I had started talking to on Plenty of Fish almost seven years earlier had told me he was from!

The Catch and Release

I woke up the next morning feeling lighter, uplifted, and determined. I knew I would give Dave one last opportunity to tell me the truth about what was going on and who he actually was. I wrote the following prayer in my journal for the day: "I pray for strength today, Lord, as I confront 'Dave.' I pray that I get the answers needed and thank You, Lord, that my life is protected and that I am loved unconditionally by You."

As I was sitting by the window in the living room, my phone next to me and my computer on my lap, I was reading, typing, and responding to Dave and others on Facebook Messenger:

8:30 a.m.	Ashlee messaged first.
8:52 a.m.	I messaged Dave.
9:03 a.m.	Dave responded.
9:25 a.m.	Dave wrote, "On plane flying home."
	I wrote, "What time are you expected to land?"
	Dave responded, "2ish."
10:01 a.m.	Sabrina messaged me.

10:16 a.m.	I wrote to Dave, "If you're flying home, you need to make a pit stop to see me."
10:18 a.m.	Dave wrote back, "I have a doctor's appointment to be at with Parker this afternoon."
10:19 a.m.	I wrote, "What time is her appointment?"
10:20 a.m.	Dave wrote, "1300. My time. Or LA time."

(If I had been in the right state of mind, I would have recognized that the time didn't add up and would have called him out on it.)

My phone started ringing from a blocked number, which I knew was Dave. Our conversation went something like this:

> "Hello."
>
> "Hey. I'm calling on the plane phone, so I can't talk for long. What's going on?"
>
> "What's going on? Why don't you tell me?"
>
> "What are you talking about?"
>
> "Dave, who are you?"
>
> "What are you talking about—who *am* I?"
>
> "I'm giving you a chance to be honest with me."
>
> "I don't know what you're talking about."
>
> "All I've ever asked for is your honesty, and I'm expecting it now. *Who are you?*"
>
> "You're being so weird, and if you're not going to tell me what's going on I'm going to hang up and we can chat more later. I have to go."
>
> "Okay. Fine. Bye." *Click.*

And that would be the last time I ever talked to or heard from Dave. He knew I knew. He knew he was caught. The one thing I don't think he knew was everything I had discovered in the last 16 or so hours:

11:43 a.m.	I checked one of the "girls'" blogs. It had the message, *Marked private as owner. Request Access or Log-out?*
12:23 p.m.	I checked Facebook. I found Dave's page to have been completely wiped clear, and Sabrina's page was all gone

with the message, *Sorry, this content isn't available right now.*

12:27 p.m. I changed my Facebook password, just to be safe.

I then went over to another close friend's house to show her everything I had just found out. While I was showing her something on my MacBook, a message popped up to call a specific number because a virus was infecting my computer. I didn't know what to do because my anxiety was already heightened with everything going on. I was clearly not thinking straight but I knew I couldn't afford to lose anything on my computer. I ended up calling the number and talking to a guy who would eventually take control of my computer. As he was trying to figure something out, I said, "I'd like full access back to my computer now. I am done with this call."

He tried to keep me on the line, though I was very forceful in telling him to get off my computer before I hung up. Later I found out that, if you have any issues with an Apple product, they will *never* have you call a number like that! *Great! Now I had to worry about this person having some of my information, too!*

PAUSE AND REFLECT

There were clearly many red flags, all of which I had chosen to ignore. I believe in the good in everyone I cross paths with. However, there always comes a point when I realize that enough is enough, that something or someone is making me feel unhealthy. Recall a time when you knew something wasn't right but didn't want to believe it right away. It could have been a family member, friend, significant other, or even a colleague who was making you feel this way.

Looking back on this time:

- What were some of the red flags you can now say you ignored?
- When did you realize that enough was enough?
- In what ways did courage play a part in confronting what you were going through?
- If you recognize you might be going through this right now, who is a trusted person you can go to for support in your next steps? A family member? Friend? Counselor? Support group? Church mentor?

Part 2
SLOW REBUILD

chapter 5

Time to Rebuild

THERE ARE MOMENTS in your life when everything around you seems to come crashing down. What do you do when this happens? You have a choice to make. Do you sit in the rubble, or do you get back up and start to rebuild, piece by piece? I chose to rebuild, and the process started the very next day.

I was sitting on the deck of another friend's house explaining everything that had happened in the last 48 hours. She looked at me and said, "Stacey, it's time to take your life back! Even though this really sucks, God has a plan for you." The next thing I knew, she was on the phone with Michelle, who had been her life coach a couple of years earlier. By the grace of God, Michelle had a cancellation that evening. I took it!

I remember pulling up to Big Boy at 7:30 p.m., not sure how this meeting would go but knowing I needed someone to talk to. More importantly, I needed help on the journey ahead.

I walked in with my notebook in hand, and the hostess pointed me to a woman in the very back booth. As I exhaled the huge breath I had been holding, I thought, *There is hardly anyone here, and we are sitting in the back, which is good, since I know the tears will be flowing freely once I begin telling her this saga.* As soon as I locked eyes with Michelle, I felt safe. The words started spilling out, and I remember telling her a few times that all of this might sound crazy but that I was going to tell it anyway.

I don't want to live in the "if onlys," nor do I want to live in the "what ifs." I've done that far too long already. I want to live in the right now, embracing each moment God gives me.

When I recently asked Michelle, who is not only a life coach but also a clinical therapist, about that first meeting, she remembered that I had expressed gratitude for being able to meet so quickly but that my energy was tied up in fear and anxiety. There were tears. Lots of tears as I began telling her about Dave and all the years of promises and dreams that had never materialized. Now, years later, Michelle recalled that she had been straightforward with me, sensing that no matter what she told me would be far better than continuing to accept the years of lies. She had been right! She told me, "You are resilient and quickly embraced the daunting emotional work ahead!"

Michelle was there to sit, lean in, write notes, and listen to all I was telling her, which in my head seemed to be like a swirling tornado! She was there. She was present. She helped me realize that it would be against the law for him to share any of the videos I had sent him and that this was not something I should fear. She also reiterated that I am not the only one who has been scammed like this and that I still have all my money! She shared with me that, in many of these situations, women send the man money and lose thousands of dollars!

Before leaving that night, we came up with the name "Scammer" to refer to this person from then on. He was no longer David, no longer Dave—no longer any name at all—because what he had done had been a scam. The title we settled on he had clearly created for himself.

Michelle and I sat there for two hours. I didn't think to ask how much she charged, but I knew that every. single. dollar would be worth it! Because I was, and still am, worth it! (Please take this as a reminder that you are, too!) I was at last aware of the web of lies; horrific deceptions; and emotional, mental, and physical abuse I had endured. I was ready to gain back control of my life and be set free!

I left the restaurant with the following playing on repeat in my mind:

I am safe.

I have all my money.

I am determined to do the work to move forward from here.

The Number *Seven*

In Scripture there is significance to the number seven, which is said to symbolize completion, healing, and the fulfillment of promises. When I look back at the timeline of my events, *seven* is indeed significant.

On May 8, 2016, I surrendered everything to God.

Seven weeks later Investigation Mode began.

Seven weeks after that I was offered a kindergarten position in West Michigan. I was moving back home!

Seven months later love bloomed again.

But before I get to that, I want you to know that those seven months were far from easy. Something like that will rock your world! Yet you have a choice. You can either bury yourself in pity and wallow in all the questions that most likely will never get answered, or you can choose to prioritize yourself and take back your life, one step at a time. I chose the latter.

I don't want to live in the "if onlys," nor do I want to live in the "what ifs." I've done that far too long already. I want to live in the right now, embracing each moment God gives me.

The next seven months brought many nights of tear-filled journal writing and life coaching sessions. Through it all, I allowed myself to recognize that, no matter how many tissues I used or how many gasps for air I took trying to catch my breath as I screamed *Why*? the investment in myself was worth it. Without allowing ourselves time to release the hurt and anger, we cannot begin the rebuilding process.

I've learned that healing is a journey not meant to be taken overnight. Even now, seven years later, I continue to journey through this healing. To be honest, I know that I will always be on this journey in some way or another because that's what trauma does to you. It shuts you down, rewires your brain, and makes you want to hide. No matter the degree to which you feel you have healed, there will always be triggers.

When I was growing up, my dad would take me and my brother to shoot skeet. I remember only one time actually hitting the moving target. Just once in all those times we went. However, I still remember the jolt of the shotgun, most of the time not knowing where the bullet would land but feeling the aftereffects of pulling that trigger in my shoulder!

Just like the bullet shot when I pulled the trigger, so a sight, smell, phrase, or name can trigger in me a blast of memories and/or emotions. The memory comes straight for you, full force, ready to shatter the moment. The jolt might hurt. It might sting. It might even knock you down, but, as with many things, over time its repetition becomes less jarring or powerful. Instead of it knocking you down, you stop it in its tracks. You validate your hurt and remind your heart that you are no longer in that space and time. That person who hurt you, who betrayed you, who took your innocence and trust, is no longer in your life, and you are still standing!

Before you rebuild, you first need to knock down the emotional walls and work to defuse the memories and their triggers. This might look different for you than it did for me. It doesn't matter how you begin; what counts is whether you begin in the first place. Journaling became a source of refuge, allowing me free rein to express my feelings, grieve, and come to terms with the loss of so much. Journaling also became one way through which I found myself talking and praying to God. Here's a sample:

September 26, 2016

I can't keep putting this off. The time I need to take for myself to sit, cry, be angry, feel hurt, scream, draw, write, and whatever else I might need to do. I feel like there's just so much he has taken from me, but on the same note, he has freed me! Seven *years*, though! *Seven!* I feel so betrayed, unwanted, and scared. I want him to leave me—leave my mind, leave my thoughts, leave my body—just *leave!* I want to erase it all. I want to find a way to turn back time and follow my intuition, my gut, which was telling me all along that something wasn't right. I just didn't listen to it.

He has taken so much from me: my time (hours upon hours), my trust, and even pieces of my body. I feel dirty, as though no one will want me. I feel as if I were held captive. I gave up so much time with my family and friends to feel as though this "fairytale" was going to end up a reality. How stupid could I be?

I'm a strong woman. How could someone treat another human the way he did? There's so much that keeps passing through my mind. Will it ever subside? Will it ever grow quiet? I want to move on. I don't want to ever think about him, the years he took from me, and the destruction he caused by manipulating and gaslighting me. I'm so angry at him! I'm angry at myself, too, for letting what he did to me literally take over my life!

I am eternally grateful for "getting out" and for the Lord coming to my rescue in my darkness and brokenness (Psalm 18). How do I truly accept what has been done to me? To innocent, naïve, kind, trustworthy, loving me? I'm sure he's not sitting around thinking about me and the mind games he played. I just wish I had let it all go years ago. The day so long ago in South Carolina when I remember last talking to him there. Why didn't I just let it go? Why did he text me when I moved back to Michigan? Why did I continue to talk to him? Why? Why? Most of all, Why *me*? He knew everything! He knew what to say. He knew how to get into my head. He knew when I was right but turned it around to make me feel as if I was the one who didn't remember, that I was the one who had a terrible memory, that I was the crazy one!

I'm so sorry, God, for things I told him about myself, my family, my friends, my life. I never did feel that I could trust him, and . . . yet again, he made me feel bad even for *that*. How do I get over this? Where do I go from here? I want to move forward and continue living my beautiful life that I'm more thankful for now than I have ever been before. But how? How can I fully heal and move on? I feel scared and defeated.

However, I also feel free, loved, and happy! How can all of these jumbled feelings coexist in me? What do I do? How do I accept the pain, the hurt, of what he's done and the way I followed and move on from all of it? When will little things stop triggering memories of what I told him, or vice versa?

He had me under his control for years. I'm scared of not being able to let in someone new for the fear of this happening again. I'm stronger because of everything I've been through, but knowing this doesn't just take it all away. He wasn't who I thought he was. Instead, he ended up being a cruel, evil, sad, and disgusting liar.

How could he just "leave" and not even try reaching out or contacting me (not that I would really want him to)? I regret ever saying "I love you" to him. I guess I loved the *idea* of him, but there exists no real-life version of him. The thought of his portraying all of those various people is just sickening. I'm sad, upset, and angry at myself for letting it go on for as long as it did—or at all!

Life isn't a fairytale or a Hallmark movie. It's tough, rough, hard, and full of mean people. I know I'm a kindhearted person who gave my time, love, and trust to someone who never deserved one ounce of it. I will never be able to retract all of my worry, stress, endless amounts of doubting, feeling crazy, and time. However, I don't want to give him, or anyone else who might have been involved, any more thought or time. I am free and want to let it go. I want to fully accept what has happened and move forward.

So, why in my heart do I still feel as though there is something holding me back? What is it? I want to officially close that chapter and continue living my life full of love, adventure, truth, trust, and the belief that everything will be okay! This new life will be better than anything I could have ever planned or imagined because I have God, my family, all my friends, a new job, a safe place to call home, and a bright future ahead!

I pray, Lord, that You help me continue to heal in a healthy way. There is a lot I feel ashamed about that I did even though I knew it wasn't right. I pray for Your forgiveness and healing grace. I can, and I will, get to the point of forgiveness, acceptance, and peace. It will take time. My heart will eventually be full of grace toward someone who was deceitful and hurt me in many ways. Thank You, Lord, for this new life, this new chapter! Please continue to bless me with Your love and goodness. Lord, I love You!

Phew! Talk about feeling all the feels! I always say that feelings are better out than in. I remember knowing that a healing night needed to occur. I was pretty stubborn at times and put off those nights because I knew they would result in a Kleenex box sitting next to me with a whole pile of snotty tissues next to it. That journal entry was from one of many such nights during those seven months. I couldn't suppress the anger, the hurt, the loss, and the grief I was going through. Interwoven throughout, though, were glimpses of hope, love, strength, and resilience. I never realized that until now.

There were, and are, always little cracks in between the spaces. No matter the size of the crack, there is only one thing that always passes through. Light. Having nights like the one I wrote about continued to break apart these hurting cracks even more, letting in more and more light.

Tears are healing. They cleanse us from the inside out. Think about the last time you cried.

- What was the reason behind the tears? A breakup? A loss? Anger? Hurt? A moment of pure joy?
- In what ways did you provide comfort for yourself during this time? Taking time to be in the moment? Journaling? Taking a hot shower? Cuddling up on the couch with your favorite blanket? Talking to a friend? Just being by yourself and giving yourself permission to cry?
- How did this comfort help you heal?

chapter 6

Rejection. Grief. Memories.

Rejection

ACCORDING TO THE online Cambridge Dictionary, *rejection* is defined as "the act of refusing to accept, use, or believe someone or something; the act of giving someone the love and attention they want and expect."

We all go through some type of rejection in our lifetime. You are not alone!

If you and I were sitting across from one another with a cup of coffee in our hands, how would you respond if I were to ask, "When in your life have you experienced or have felt rejection?" Would you talk about the time you were cut from a team? Would you share about the time your significant other told you they didn't see themselves with you anymore? Would you talk about when you thought you'd had the best interview for your dream job, only to get the call that they had chosen someone else? We all go through some type of rejection in our lifetime. You are not alone!

As I was journaling one day, I began to discover a root cause of my pain—rejection. Here's what I wrote:

> Part of this week I was trying to be aware of what I just can't seem to let go of regarding Scammer. I think it's because I'm afraid to be myself, in person, around someone I like. The phone and computer are both ways to not fully expose myself. I will talk to anyone, but as I reflect, I am recognizing that when I am interested in someone in the flesh, I clam up. Then I regret not saying anything to them. I think it's because I fear being rejected. I may not be what they want or are looking for. Who could love me and want to be only with me? I know I'm a godly woman, but I'm afraid of rejection because of things I've been through and things I've done. Why open myself up, only to be let down, dumped, and hurt in the end? My wall of protection has been rebuilt. I tried letting it down when I was talking to Scammer, but in the end this left me devastated and broken. I felt used. I am realizing that I have dated online because it has been a way to hide myself before meeting anyone in person.

Oh, the narratives we create in our minds that crush our souls. The stories we create in our minds are just that—stories. Stories that lead to our rejection of our worth, our compassion, and our love for who we are! Why do we do this to ourselves?

Instead of asking why, start telling yourself, "I'm not the only one!" Because you aren't. Begin believing that the rejection is only leading you to something better. Because it is.

We all deserve to feel wanted and loved. Do you have doubts that creep in, as I do at times, telling you otherwise? If so, recite this prayer:

> *I pray, Lord, that You will take away any doubt I might be struggling with in my heart. Give me Your Word to read and remind me daily that I am loved. I am strong. I am a Child of God. I am me, and that's more than enough!*

Grief

Grief is defined by Merriam-Webster Dictionary as "deep and poignant distress caused by or as if by bereavement." There are many different ways to think about grief, but one thing we need to remember is that grief is personal. No two people grieve in the same way, nor do we grieve on the same timeline. Grief is not something you "go through" in a certain amount of time. It is a process, and there will be waves of grief throughout our lives. It's not like in a movie where the actress gets hurt but a couple of months later finds her "true" love . . . and the rest is history. That is not real life. It's important for me to write and talk about the grief, hurt, abuse, and healing because it's all part of the process. A process that doesn't happen overnight or even over a few months, but instead over years!

> I pray that God hears my cries for healing. Last night, I spent 2+ hours deleting photos from my phone from Scammer. I even relistened to the voicemails he left. *Delete.* I started off with tears, but as I was deleting the photos I felt a sense of freedom. Tears came with the voicemails, but they were tears of "How could someone do this?" This is all part of my past, and although I want to forget all the parts with Scammer, they will always be part of me. I want to be free of the thoughts and triggers and of knowing how much time, heartache, and energy he took from me. He was a lesson, nothing more. He was a lesson I've learned from. I want someone who treats me right, sees me for me, communicates, makes me feel special, loves me unconditionally, and sees and accepts my flaws . . . and vice versa. The only One who can make this happen is God.
>
> When I reached out to Michelle about deleting Scammer's number, along with all the notes I'd had in my phone, she responded by writing, "Yep, it is time to catch your dreams, and you can't when you're loaded down with grief . . . Let it go!" So, I did!
>
> I pray for continued healing. I pray that I take the time to cry and allow myself moments to sob. Michelle also reminded me to "Cry as much as you need! You are grieving the loss of fantasy and the betrayal of reality. When you are ready, embrace the possibilities

> that are to come true and that you so well deserve!" I am ready to embrace these possibilities head on. I pray for the love, support, and guidance to have an open heart and mind for whatever is to come for my future!

Vicki Harrison describes grief very well: "Grief is like the ocean; it comes on waves, ebbing and flowing. Sometimes the water is calm and sometimes it is overwhelming. All we can do is learn to swim."

I couldn't agree more! We all need time and space to ebb and flow in and out of grief. I needed to take time to grieve the loss of the fantasy world Scammer had gaslighted me into, along with the betrayal of all I felt I had lost. This would take time. I knew the healing would come in waves. At this point in my journey, although I was grieving especially the loss of love, I felt hopeful for the love that was surrounding me every day—the love I still believed in.

During this time in 2016, while I was experiencing grief and on my healing journey, I told Michelle and a few close friends that God had put it on my heart to write a book someday. The purpose of the book would be to talk openly about what I've experienced to help other women with similar experiences feel less alone. The book you are reading right now is intended to remind you of two things:

1. You are far from alone.
2. Everyone has a story.

Our story makes each of us who we are, and it's about time we embrace our own and each other's stories! By doing so, we can walk alongside others as we all ride the waves of grief, creating new memories as we swim along.

Memories

Dictionary.com defines *memory* as "the mental capacity or faculty of retaining and reviving facts, events, impressions, etc., or of recalling or recognizing previous experiences."

Retaining. Reviving. Recalling.

Memories are a part of us. Some memories are like shadows that sweep by every so often without much detail. However, some memories have been wired into our brains due to our having replayed the conversation or event over and over again. Some of these memories we'd like to rewire to become shadow memories without the vivid details. Others, though, we want to hold onto forever.

I remember the day I drove to my parents' house on the lake, four days after everything had surfaced with Scammer. I was about to tell my mom what had happened. One of the hardest things I went through was feeling secluded from my family and friends during the final year and a half of being manipulated. It was challenging for my family and friends to talk to me about any of this. I was defending a relationship that I felt deep down wasn't right, but I brushed it off and reassured everyone that everything was fine. I knew that, no matter what, my parents just wanted me to be safe. They both, and especially my mom, knew that I wasn't. However, she didn't know what to do or how to talk to me about it. The truth was that I wasn't at the point of being able or willing to listen. I defended myself instead.

I have always been able to go to my mom for advice, encouragement, and support, and she is one of my best friends. She knew that I would be moving to California not just for a job but to find out what this relationship I had told her about would bring.

Memory Recall:

I remember the look in my mom's eyes at Christmas 2015 when she gave me and my brother pillows from a local artist. My brother's had Michigan painted on his, and mine had California. With tears in her eyes, she said, "California is your next dream." That meant the world to me because it was her way of telling me that she was slowly accepting my upcoming move. This was also the Christmas when my parents bought me a purple luggage set—which had, ironically, been suggested by Scammer and Sabrina. I remember the smiles and the photo I had my mom take, which I later sent to Scammer.

I remember driving at a snail's pace up the long dirt road to my parents' house, my stomach in knots—the type of knots you get when you feel guilty about having done something you knew wasn't right, but that you did anyway and now have to admit. Deep down, I probably felt guilty because I hadn't listened to them. I never wanted to hear what they had to say because I had a narcissist telling me lies, gaslighting me into thinking and feeling the way he wanted me to think and feel and trying to turn all my support against me.

I think that, when Scammer started to realize that my loved ones weren't going anywhere, his game started to falter. The guilty knots were entangling and wrapping themselves around me, making me feel like a little girl who just wanted her mom. I needed my mom to hug me, to hold me, and to assure me that everything was going to be okay.

I pulled up to the house as my mom came out to greet me. As soon as we locked eyes through the windshield, I could tell she knew something was wrong. I got out of the car and started walking toward her saying, "Mom, I have to tell you something." She embraced me, and I knew she wanted to protect me in any way she could. I burst into tears, and she held me as we walked inside. We sat on the couch by the window facing the lake, her body tight against mine. Holding my hand, she asked with concern on her face, "Stacey, what's wrong?"

"I was scammed."

"What? Are you okay? I knew it! Ugh! I had a feeling. I knew something wasn't right! Are you okay?"

"Yes, I will be, but it's going to take time."

I told her a lot of what had happened. She listened and held me. And, just as when I was a little girl, I felt safe and knew I would be okay.

During this time memories were also surfacing in the form of dreams. One December afternoon I came home and took a nap. I dreamed that I was catching a flight to go somewhere, but I couldn't find the gate. When I finally found it, I learned that the flight had been cancelled. When I went to the ticket counter, the lady informed me that the ticket I had was a scam. I started to cry. She said, "We've had a couple of other girls go through this recently." She booked me on a flight back to Detroit the next morning. Worried about not having enough money for a hotel, I got into the car rental line and at some point saw my mom. I ran to give her a huge hug! Then I woke up.

This dream spliced together everything I had been going through for the past few months:

- The desire to actually meet someone I had been talking to for almost seven years.
- Realizing it was all a scam.
- Trying to get a vehicle to drive me away from it all.
- Still having all my money.
- Landing in the sweet, safe embrace of my mom.

Even months after the final piece had happened, my brain was still trying to sort it all out. Bottom line, though, I was safe.

The months that followed included a lot of healing, accompanied by many tears and my giving myself permission to enjoy the penny moments of life. What is a penny moment? We all know that a penny is just one cent, such a small amount that we discount its value. However, when you collect pennies and add them up, you begin to realize how valuable each one is. Many pennies can add up to great wealth! You just have to be open to saving them. A couple of things about penny moments:

- They are small.
- They are often missed as we rush to get to the next thing.
- When you don't notice the penny moments, your inner critic, negative thoughts, and toxicity might set in. However, when you take time to sit, think about, and collect them, penny moments add up to the blessing called life.

The next months were full of penny moments, including:

- Going to bed at 8:42 p.m. because no one was telling me I was an "old lady" for going to sleep so early. (This is what I was often told by Scammer.)
- Lying on my couch sipping coffee, wrapped in the blanket my mom had made for me, reading my devotional and feeling at peace.
- Giggles from my students as "Miss Holiday" took them on adventures celebrating and learning about the many different *Holidays around the World*.
- Taking naps.

- Wrangling my kindergartners on stage for our Snow Show and watching them sing their little hearts out as they looked around for their moms and dads.
- Making and decorating Christmas cookies with my mom and brother, as we had done when we were kids.
- Bundling up for the cold Michigan weather and going out to build a snowman.
- The joy, laughter, and love surrounding me while opening Christmas presents and reflecting on where I had been a year earlier.
- Running up and down the basketball court again, this time as a coach.
- Being invited to a book club, where I was introduced to my next boyfriend.

Think about one of your penny moments. One that might not be worth mentioning to someone else but that makes you feel whole and complete! Write it down and think about:

- Who was a part of it?
- What specific details of that moment made it so special?

chapter 7

Relationships after Trauma

WE WERE CREATED for relationship. God knew from the beginning that humans need each other, whether in friendship or romantically. We are not meant to do life alone (Genesis 2:18).

A relationship . . .

- Builds over time.
- Is a connection to someone with similar values, morals, beliefs, and interests.
- Is built on trust, love, and respect.
- Is knowing that, even though someone may not intend to hurt you, they may do so . . . and then be able to apologize and admit they were wrong (and vice versa).
- Is vulnerable.
- Can be romantic or between friends, acquaintances, coworkers, neighbors, or family members.
- Can be scary and risky.
- Can be temporary.

- » Can be broken.
- » Can be on a surface level, intimate, or deep.
- » Can be beautiful.

How do you know you're ready to be in a romantic relationship once again after heartbreak or deceit? I don't know that there is a timeline. Though I was grateful to be living abundantly and freely, I felt as though there were some void in me that still needed to be filled. I began praying for my future husband and even listed everything I wanted in him.

I continue to pray for a husband who . . .

- » Is a godly Christian man.
- » Attends church and serves others.
- » Has a strong spiritual, emotional, mental, and physical moral compass.
- » Is respectful to others and to me.
- » Shows me how special I am.
- » Cares about and is kind to everyone around him.
- » Is family oriented.
- » Wants children of his own some day.
- » Appreciates the little things.
- » Knows and admits when he's wrong.
- » Is independent.
- » Is secure.
- » Gives of his time.
- » Accepts and loves me for me—my past, present, and future.
- » Is forgiving and talks openly about things.
- » Is a handyman.
- » Is at least 6' 2" tall.
- » Is athletic and adventurous.
- » Is sarcastic at the appropriate times.
- » Knows when to be serious and when to laugh and have fun.

How many of you have made such a list? This was an updated list. My first one was written on a neon pink 3 x 5 notecard years ago; it included the top ten things I was looking for in a guy at that time. I remember thinking that I would love to have all ten but that eight out of ten would be pretty good, and I'd take that! Well, that list went from ten to twenty, and, if I'm being honest seven years later, it is still evolving. I believe this is because I have learned from dating relationships along the way. After I went through my dating Ferris wheel years ago, I began wanting to date for the purpose of marriage. But how long do you keep dating someone when you realize that enough is enough? My goal is less than seven years!

Greg

One of my former college roommates, Kennedy, had mentioned someone back in December 2016 whom one of her fellow doctors knew. They both wanted to set us up. I had gotten to know this doctor's wife, Stella, a bit, and in February 2017 Stella invited me to a book club she was in. I understood that the main reason behind the invite was for me to meet this guy. As I got ready for the evening, a case of nerves started to kick in. I kept telling myself, *It's just a time to meet new friends. That's all, Stace. Go, have fun!*

Kennedy and I drove to the house together and were greeted by two familiar faces—Stella and her husband—along with several others. I made myself a drink and started to mingle. Greg had come in with his sister and her husband. I could tell right away that his sister had a fun personality and that, if nothing else, she and I would become instant friends. Greg and I were awkwardly introduced to one another before we moved into the living room to continue to chat. It was fun to drink, laugh, and get to know new people. Greg and I exchanged numbers before Kennedy and I left. As we got into her car, I said, "I definitely am interested and would be up for going out with him." She smiled and drove me home.

I didn't hear from Greg for a few days, so, after overthinking the situation, I texted him. Not surprisingly, I didn't hear back from him right away, but he did eventually respond, and we met at the Downtown Market on Sunday. I enjoyed our time and looked forward to seeing him again.

We spent the next several days talking, cooking dinner, watching movies and episodes of *Grey's Anatomy*, and getting to know one another. I prayed daily for patience, especially because I knew he was still going to therapy sessions with his ex. I was hopeful and optimistic but also had a gut feeling that I should give him time. There were many times when I ignored that gut feeling, even when I could feel it lingering. I highly recommend not doing this!

One evening Greg asked me what had happened in June. I was open and revealed in-depth details of what I had gone through. He listened. He was there. He showed me that he cared and reassured me that he thought it was refreshing and incredible that I was still full of life, love, and faith, even after such antics. As I left his house that night, I felt freer and more accepted after having been so vulnerable with someone I was interested in.

Greg and I spent the weekends going to Holland and Grand Haven, both along the Lake Michigan shoreline, taking our first photo together at Lake Michigan, continuing our long talks until the wee hours of the morning, and going to church together on Sunday.

One Sunday Greg asked if I wanted to go to his aunt's house for lunch. I was welcomed there with love and felt so comfortable. He came from a loving, fun Christian family. The time we spent together strengthened our friendship/relationship.

In March, Greg surprised me with a beautiful plant. I remember feeling so special that he had thought about me and actually bought me a plant rather than flowers. "A plant lasts longer," he told me. Another surprise I received that day was a kiss! I hadn't kissed anyone for at least two years, since I had committed to seeing what Scammer and I might have had. The chemistry between me and Greg was definitely there! The next several days brought so many emotions. I had to get used to the fact that Greg had recently gotten a new job and was working out of town a lot during the week. So, our time together was mostly on the weekends. As I felt more and more of a connection with Greg, I thought of 1 Corinthians 13:4–7 (MSG):

> Love never gives up.
> Love cares more for others than for self.
> Love doesn't want what it doesn't have.
> Love doesn't strut,

Doesn't have a swelled head,
Doesn't force itself on others,
Isn't always 'me first,'
Doesn't fly off the handle,
Doesn't keep score of the sins of others,
Doesn't revel when others grovel,
Takes pleasure in the flowering of truth,
Puts up with anything,
Trusts God always,
Always looks for the best,
Never looks back,
But keeps going to the end.

Love is from the Lord, who will always supply us with the love we need. The question surfacing for me was, *When do you know if it's true love*? One night as Greg was leaving and we kissed, I almost said, "I love you." But was it love? What does it mean and feel like to truly be in love? Will we know when we are in love? You're not alone if you have asked these same questions.

Our feelings for one another and our intimacy kept building. Despite the wonderings starting to creep in, the joy was there. I took it day by day, embracing every moment Greg and I spent together. It was all real. It was all in-person. And it was something I hadn't experienced in a long time.

For the next couple of months, Greg and I continued to build our relationship and spent every weekend together. One night his ex was weighing heavily on my mind. I expressed that I was a little scared that she would realize she had made a terrible mistake and want him back. He listened and reassured me that I had nothing to worry about. During this time I prayed for patience, peace, and the guarding of my heart. I found myself praying for Greg's ex as well, that she would discover who she was and learn from the relationship she'd had with Greg. I also prayed for Greg and me, that we would continue to be open, honest, and truthful with each other, no matter what.

Though my relationship with Greg was a springboard to feeling desired by another person, the triggers and memories were still there. However, as I lived in the present moment and with a stronger sense of reality, those memories started to fade. There will always be times, though, that thoughts and feelings still surface.

Change is part of life. Although it can be hard at times, it is necessary. And sometimes change happens when you least expect it.

There were a couple of Sundays I remember spending with Greg that continued to help my healing. The first was the afternoon Greg and I took a short road trip to where I had grown up. As we sat in the car talking, I began to cry. There were so many feelings surfacing as we talked. Greg told me that he appreciated my tender heart, and this broke open the floodgates even more. He saw the part of me that had been criticized in the past about being too sensitive and emotional. This moment with Greg comforted my heart and made me feel seen and validated.

The second instance was a Sunday in May. We were sitting together in church listening to a sermon about manipulators, which, as you can imagine, hit very close to home for me. That sermon brought up memories of things Scammer had done and/or of how he had made me feel, and I found myself with tears streaming down my face as I listened. Greg took my hand at one point and held it. This little action made me feel safe and less alone. When we were walking out, he commented, "That message was hard for you to hear." I once again felt seen and explained that the next month and a half would bring some emotional times because I was nearing the one-year anniversary of the reality with Scammer surfacing. Greg was there. And he stayed . . . until he didn't.

Change is part of life. Although it can be hard at times, it is necessary. And sometimes change happens when you least expect it.

I never took spending time with Greg for granted because during the week he regularly traveled for work. When we were together, we took walks, lay in hammocks at the park, took bike rides, and went to church and out for brunch afterward. Sundays always brought sadness because I knew I wouldn't see him again until Friday. It never crossed my mind to wonder about who he might be talking to or who might be contacting him during the week. I never had any doubts because I trusted him.

One Sunday, though, after returning home from a weekend with friends on the east side of the state, Greg came over, and I could feel in my gut that something was up. It was a feeling I'd had all weekend, though I had been trying not to overthink the situation. He told me that he had in fact been talking to his ex (straight punch to the gut, pretty much knocking all the trust out of me) and that she wanted to try things again because she realized she had made a huge mistake.

This was precisely what I had been afraid of and the apprehension I had expressed to Greg toward the beginning of our talking. Remember his response at the time? He had assured me that I had nothing to worry about. Oh, if only I had listened to my gut back then! (I've come to realize that there's always a reason for these gut feelings.) Yet without vulnerability, trust, hope, and putting yourself out there, you risk never experiencing love. And what kind of life would that be? My feelings of sadness, disappointment, and heartbreak were running strong. All I could do was pray.

> *I pray, Lord, that You will give me the strength, peace, love in my heart, and hope that I need to move on. That I can be brave. That I can be hopeful in what You, Lord, have planned for my life. The only man I can fully trust with my whole heart, my whole mind, and my whole soul is You. Please guide me through the day, getting me through without too many tears.*

The morning after Greg's revelation, I received on my way to school a text from Greg: "Good morning, Stacey. I want you to know that you are in my prayers and on my heart. I pray that you have a good day!" I responded by thanking him for writing, assuring him that he was also in my prayers, and admitting that Monday was also a rough day for me.

His response was: "Aww! Yesterday was really hard for me, too! My heart was aching. I'm definitely struggling, and I pray that God reveals. Please know that I care about you very much! God will guide both of us. He never lets us down!" I found myself hoping that we would get back together someday.

That week brought a lot of tears, along with writing, praying, and trying to understand. The thing is that there are times when, no matter how much you try to understand, you just can't.

As Marjorie Vawter writes in *Encouraging Thoughts for Women: Hope*, "Hope isn't just an emotion; it's a perspective, a discipline, a way of life. It's a journey of choice. Hope is smiling in the darkness. It's confidence that faith in God's sovereignty amounts to something . . . something life-changing, lifesaving, and eternal."

I wrote a letter to Greg to help me process my feelings. Here's part of it:

> I have loved the adventures we have already taken, and I looked forward to the adventures ahead with you. I don't want to lose you or lose us. You make me an even happier woman just being with you. What I want to say is, "Choose me. Be with me. Love me." But I also know you and respect you for being honest. I want to give you the time you need to figure out what your heart wants. I care for you very much and want you to be happy—you deserve that. I miss you. I keep praying and hoping that one of these days you will be at my door, ready to make our relationship work . . . for you to be "all-in" with me.

Do you recognize the quote in that letter? Yes, it's *Grey's Anatomy* at its finest! Someone should have reminded me that just like movies, shows tend to be unrealistic as well; for the next ten months I was living in my own little drama!

The next month brought a lot of texts and calls with Greg, and we even met up at the park to talk about things. This period of time also brought a lot of confusion and a few sessions with Michelle. She encouraged me to limit my "wait time" to two months—definitely no more than three. She even encouraged me to take a risk and tell him that I would still love to go camping with him over the Fourth of July. I took the risk. Nothing ventured, nothing gained, right? No matter how much this sucked, no matter how much it hurt, and no matter the amount of confusion, I still had something pulling on my heart and telling me to hold on—that this was the man I was going to marry. I felt hopeful.

The Fourth of July was quickly approaching. The night before heading to my parents' for the week, I cried out to God in my journal:

> I am feeling hurt, sad, and a little bit angry. Greg told me he was hoping to meet up with his ex to discuss and see "where her head's at." I feel the most hurt that I've been throughout this process because I haven't heard from him yet. For all I know, they could be up north camping together. I also had the thought that maybe they didn't meet up last night and will be doing so today or tonight instead.
>
> I'm in the land of overthinking and wondering, and as a result I'm driving myself crazy! I kind of feel like I did with Scammer: always unsure, not knowing, and second-guessing. I don't want to ever feel that way again and am angry at myself for that! I will continue to pray for Greg's clarity and my own patience and strength, along with some type of closure soon. I pray that I won't leave anything unsaid. That's hard because I'm holding onto our memories and our time together. It has been weeks since we've actually been the way we were before all of this surfaced.
>
> It's just so unfair! I've done nothing wrong, and although I appreciate his honesty and respect his needing to heal and figure it all out, I'm hurt. I'm frustrated. I don't know what to do or where to go from here. I know the Lord will provide and it will all end up according to His plan, but I have to be honest: it sucks right now! I want to go back to the time before his ex came back into the picture. It's. not. fair! How can she be the one to walk away and then want him back when she realizes how stupid she was for letting him go? And now he is trying to figure out if that was just a "crazy time" for her. I'm *me*! I've always been *myself*! And no matter how frustrating all of this is, I do love him.

I encourage you to express your feelings somehow, especially when something big happens. Write it out, yell it out, talk to a friend, but just get it out somehow! These emotions do no good lingering inside you. Doing so will help you release emotions buried deep within. I've noticed that, once those emotions are out in the universe, there is no telling what will happen in the days that follow.

After getting all of this out, I drove to my parents' lake house, where my brother and I were planning to spend the week building end tables for my living room. I had mustered up the courage to respond to a text Greg had sent. I was honest and told him that, although I didn't want to write everything in a text, I didn't know when I would be able to talk to him on the phone or see him in person again. I felt that he needed to know how I was feeling.

That day, my brother and I went to Menard's to pick up the wood for my end tables. When we got home, I looked at my phone, and there was a text from Greg: "Hi cutie pie (his nickname for me). God revealed what needed to be revealed to me about my ex. It's over, and I'm ready to put this behind me and move forward with you. I am still up north in Traverse City and would love for you to join me for the next couple days. I'll understand if you don't want to, considering everything that has happened."

I remember my heart fluttering and the butterflies scurrying about as I read the text. I rushed downstairs to show my mom. We were standing in the kitchen, and when she was finished reading it, she asked, "What are you going to do?" Everything in my heart was telling me to *go!*

After talking to my mom, I decided to risk it and go! I texted him back, hopped in the shower, and got ready. I called him before I left. No answer. I left him a message that I was on my way. I thought it was odd that he hadn't answered yet. I remember hugging my mom goodbye as she told me to have fun. As I drove off, my gut was telling me, *I think you should wait until you hear back from him.* Do you think I listened? Nope. I drove the hour and forty-five minutes north without hearing from him.

I knew the campground he was at but didn't know which site. So, since I still hadn't heard from him, I decided to drive around to see whether I could find it. As I was driving as slowly as a snail trying to spot his tent, I saw him. He was talking to someone. There sitting on a cooler was . . . his ex.

My window was down, and I think he saw me. I didn't know what to do. My stomach instantly dropped. I thought I was going to throw up and shit my pants at the same time! I kept driving, parked at the beach parking lot, and called my friend. I then called Greg, left him another message, texted him, and still . . . nothing. I sat there speechless, shaking and unable to move. *What do I do now? Should I wait until he answers? Should I just drive back home?* (Yes, Stacey, this is exactly what you should have done!)

Incoming call. It was him.

I answered. I could tell he was distressed and that it had been an emotional day for him. He met me at the beach parking lot because my stomach was upset and I knew I had to use the bathroom. When I walked out of the restroom, there he was, sitting on the picnic table. I walked over, still shaking. We talked. A lot. I was open and honest with him.

I shouldn't have stayed. I realize that now, but I had hope for us. I wanted us to move forward and be a stronger couple because of all of this. At that moment, in my eyes, he had chosen me.

We went out to dinner, and when we got back to the campsite I remember looking at the tent and thinking, *I can only imagine what his neighbors must be thinking. One girl one night, another the next.* I looked at Greg and asked, "Did you and your ex have sex in that tent?" He said, "No, that was one of the major issues. She hasn't had the passion for me like she did before. We became more like friends and not intimate partners." In my vulnerable state I trusted him, and I stayed.

The next couple of days were spent talking, hiking Sleeping Bear Dunes, going to Glen Arbor, and reconnecting. So much so that we did end up having sex. Being in his arms again made me feel hopeful.

On our way out of Traverse City, we stopped at a winery. I remember getting into our separate cars as I drove back to my parents' house, and I had tears in my eyes. I was filled with so many emotions! I was happy, I was still hesitant, and I wanted to pinch myself as I kept asking, *Is this really happening*?

I texted my friend Joe. I have always referred to Joe as my "Hitch" (yes, from the movie). Joe has been there through a lot of my dating extravaganza, has coached me along the way, and has seen me grow as a person, especially regarding relationships. He also is protective because he knows how guys work, and he knows my heart. He asked me a question I couldn't answer because I didn't *know* the answer. His question was, "So, is he all in?" This question really got me thinking. I wasn't sure if Greg was all in, and I knew I needed to ask him. (Hello again, gut!)

Greg would be leaving for Italy for two weeks to train for his new job, and I wanted to drive him to the airport. I woke up in the morning having heard nothing from him. Still nothing as I drove home. At 2:00 p.m. he called. He told me that his power had gone out and that he had called me as soon as it had come back on. Looking back, I remember thinking, *Hmm . . . was your cell phone not charged?* Which, knowing him, it might not have been. Shortly afterward I picked him up.

As we drove to the airport, I felt in my stomach that I needed to ask him before he left.

He was rolling his suitcase as I carried a big manila envelope, a travel package I had made him for his trip. Inside were some of his favorite goodies, along with cards I had written to him that he could open on certain days or whenever he felt like it. We were walking in when I stopped him. I looked at him and said, "There's something I have to ask you. You took this time to find out if your ex was all in with you, but I never thought to ask you if *you*, now, are all in with me." His response was not what I wanted to hear, but it was what my gut had been trying to warn me about all along.

He responded that he couldn't fully tell me he was one hundred percent all in because his ex was not stopping. She was now trying to "fight" for him. He was ninety percent in with me, but there was that ten percent of which he still felt he couldn't let go. I stood there thinking, *Are you kidding me?* He told me that he didn't want to keep pulling me onto this roller coaster and wanted me to move forward because I deserved so much better.

I handed him his travel package and said, "Here, I put this together for you, and you might as well have it." I looked him in the eye and said, "You are going to lose me, and I don't want that. What you are doing to me is what your ex is doing to you. Have a safe flight." I don't recall hugging him but instead walked away, got in my car, and screamed over and over, "*Why?*"

Why, God?

Why did You put him into my life, only to take him away?

Why can't he just let her go?

Why can't his ex leave him alone?

Why is this happening when I've done nothing wrong?

I don't know how to fully express my feelings and emotions:

Frustrated that he has hurt me again.

Frustrated that another relationship has ended.

Angry that I made the choice to spend time with him when I should have stayed with my family. (Lesson learned: Family is always first! If a man loves and cares about you, he will understand that.)

Hurt that he is not "all in" with me. He said that he never wanted me to get hurt, but what did he expect would happen?

Sad that he is letting go of all we were building, all our happy times and the memories we've shared.

Calm and *at peace*, which is a little weird to admit because I feel and know that I am, and will be, okay.

Stronger because of this time, process, and relationship.

I wish I could say it all ended there. I wish I could tell you that I moved on. I wish I could tell you that I said, "Your loss, Greg!" But I can't. There were months of continued back and forth, reflection, tears, overthinking, and many prayers every single day.

PAUSE AND REFLECT

Think about a relationship you have had in which, when you reflect on it now, you realize that there were certain behaviors, actions, or thoughts you chose to ignore because you just wanted it to work.

- List these behaviors, actions, and thoughts and consider how you might have responded differently, knowing what you know now.
- What lesson(s) did you learn from this relationship?

chapter 8

What You're Never Told about Love

NO ONE TELLS you love is easy.

No one tells you love takes time.

No one tells you love hurts.

No one tells you love is hard.

No one tells you love breaks you down.

No one tells you that you have to find a way to continue to build yourself back up after a loss of love, whether it's from a mother, father, grandparent, friend, lover, coworker, or child.

No one tells you that love leads to broken hearts along the way.

Love doesn't stop. There will always be a little love left over for the person, no matter how much they have hurt you. The person is someone you've spent time with, built memories with and, if you were sexually intimate, someone who will always have a part of you. We all have basic survival needs, and one of these is love! We need to feel loved, be loved, show love, embrace love, and cherish love. Giving love is free, but too often people offer things that aren't free, causing heartache in the long run.

But our hearts are teachable. We need a teachable heart to learn the lessons love tries to show us along the way. God leads us from one place to another. Why? To mature us and bring us to where He wants us to be. Letting go is one of the hardest things for us to do. I know that I find it challenging to do so and that I am still learning that letting go is necessary for me to continue healing. Letting go doesn't mean forgetting, but it will lead you to a space closer to where you belong.

Everyone knows the saying "Time heals all wounds." It does to a certain extent, but when trust is broken, when there is a lack of communication back and forth and so much uncertainty, those wounds may never fully heal.

When rereading my journals from this time, I recognized that I often wrote about the unknown, the uncertainty, the hesitation. It ultimately came down to trust. I had waited. I'd had moments to reflect about living the single life, though this had felt more like living a limbo single life, since Greg and I had kept in touch on and off and had seen each other at church now and then. I'd be lying if I said I never wanted to see him again. Every time I turned into the parking lot at church, I hoped his car would be there. This limbo life had brought with it nights of tears, confusion, and wondering. The one verse from Scripture in which I found comfort during this time was Psalm 56:8 (NLT): "You keep track of all of my sorrows. You have collected all my tears in your bottle. You have recorded each one in your book."

Close your eyes. Envision a beautiful jar in which all of your tears from every emotion—joy, sadness, hurt, despair, anger, confusion, grief, love—are collected and held, cleansing your soul from within. How does this make you feel?

In October Greg and I reconnected more often. We went on bike rides and out to dinner; watched MSU games together; and, yet again, rebuilt something that had already been broken twice. However, there was always an underlying fear that the relationship could end. He could easily choose her again, leaving me feeling unwanted.

At the end of October, I asked him to tell me if or when his ex had texted him. He told me that she had. (Hello, gut—oh, how I've missed you. Or have you never really left?) He said he hadn't answered her but that, if he did, he would tell her, "It's over, and I've moved on." When I asked him if she knew about me, he said yes.

Looking back, I realize that I should have handled this conversation differently. If I could respond now, I would stay curious about what he was expressing. I would ask him why he hadn't told her this already. I would have wanted his actions to speak more loudly than his words.

Fast forward to December, when I spent Christmas in Florida with my family. Greg drove me to the airport. I was about to get into the TSA line when we hugged and he said, "I love you!" I remember thinking, *Wait, did he just say what I think he said?* We kissed, and as I walked away I remember thinking, *He just said "I love you" for the first time!* I felt like I was on cloud nine! That was the best Christmas gift I could have asked for from him! Before we took off, I sent him a text asking if I had heard him correctly. I didn't get an answer until I turned my phone back on when I landed: "No need to replay the 'see you soon' scene. I love you! There are plenty of them to come!"

I spent the holidays with my family, enjoying our time together. On my return home, Greg's sister was planning to pick me up from the airport, since Greg was supposed to be out of town for work. As I walked down the ramp expecting to see her, I saw Greg instead! This was the best surprise!

At the start of 2018, we decided to take our first weeklong vacation together during my spring break. We chose Punta Cana, the Dominican Republic. At the end of January, I was talking to my mom about how we had booked the trip. I remember her telling me that this was a huge "test," since we would be together for a whole week. I hadn't thought about that until she mentioned it. I laughed and responded, "No pressure or anything!"

I began looking for a swimsuit for spring break; I decided to look on Pinterest and typed in "reasonable bathing suit." Up popped a picture of my former friend "Sabrina," who was the swimsuit model. I didn't know how to feel and didn't want to cry, but the tears came anyway. I was texting a friend at the time, and she was telling me about how one of her clients was going through Snapchat bullying. (Scammer had made me believe that Snapchat was dangerous and warned me never to go on it.) I told my friend about the picture of

"Sabrina," and she encouraged me to seek legal action because she feared that Scammer was a serial abuser. I explained to her again why I hadn't done just that. I had known that moments like this would happen. Although triggers are a part of trauma, they are also a component of healing. I let the tears fall, knowing they were cleansing me and helping me move forward.

At the end of March, it was time to spend a whole week with the man I loved! On March 31, 2018, after only three hours of sleep, Greg and I woke up at 4:00 a.m. to head to the airport. I wrote in my journal while flying and prayed that we would have an amazing trip, full of new memories together.

I was so happy being in this beautiful place with the warm sun on my skin and the ocean breeze surrounding us. Our days were filled with walks on the beach, bottomless drinks, fresh fruit, soaking up the sun at the pools, and lots of laughter and conversations together. On one of our first mornings, we went for a walk on the beach without sunglasses or sunscreen. Needless to say, I got burned and had to stay out of the sun for a day or two. Such a Michigan girl mistake!

We both had been to all-inclusive resorts before, but I felt that Greg was constantly comparing this resort to the one he had gone to in Mexico after initially taking a break from his ex. The mojitos were better there, the chairs comfier, the rooms more modern, and the service and shows better. I mentioned a couple of things I remembered from the resorts I had been to, but I wasn't fixated on comparing, and I started getting tired of his doing so. He came off as complaining that this place wasn't as good as his earlier experience. I shouldn't have taken this personally, but I did, because the difference with this experience was that I was a part of it.

We all have moments when our significant other says something that hits us in an unexpected way. This happened one afternoon when Greg and I were at the pool, drinking our tropical beverages. I was telling him about the novel I was reading, *The Ten Best Days of My Life* by Adena Halpern, in which the main character recalls the ten best days of her life. One was getting married and starting a family. When I told Greg about this part, he responded that, if he ever got married and had kids, it would have to be with the right person. I tried to keep the tears from welling (I'm sure it didn't help that I had frozen mojitos in my bloodstream). His words made me feel as though maybe he didn't want to get married someday . . . or, rather, that he didn't want to marry me!

Greg asked me about my parents and their marriage. I kept it short by saying that, although my parents, as with every relationship, have their ups and downs, I know they love one another. Do I learn about what I may desire in a marriage someday by watching my parents and other family members, friends, and couples? Yes! I think that most people learn from observing relationships and marriages of people they know and figuring out what they envision their own marriage looking and feeling like someday.

I found myself slowly shutting down and becoming quieter as the afternoon continued. When we returned to the room, I hopped into the shower and cried. I remember standing under the flowing water trying not to make too much noise so Greg wouldn't know. Why was I crying? I'm pretty sure it was because my gut was telling me to be careful and be on guard.

We started our last day in the Dominican by watching the sunrise. It was nice to take photos prior to the hustle and bustle the day would bring. It was all so calming, especially the sound of the ocean waves. When we got back, Greg and I sat on the patio together. I was feeling sad that our time away was ending, but I knew that every vacation draws to a close. We wouldn't appreciate vacations as much if they didn't. I didn't know what stepping back into reality would mean as I faced the next seven days. (There's that number *seven* again.)

Our trip was special, and I enjoyed every moment. This was the first time in a long time that I hadn't thought about Greg and his ex. It was just us! However, as we were standing in the airport waiting for our layover flight, we both turned on our phones after having left them off all week. My gut turned right back on along with my phone, and the anxiousness returned full force. Greg was looking for his aunt's number to text her that we were back in the States. As I glanced over at his phone, I thought I saw his ex's name before my own on his text messages. To be honest, I don't know this for certain, but I do remember that the familiar feelings of worry quickly crept back in.

We didn't get back into town until 11:30 p.m. and back to Greg's house till around midnight, after which he drove me home. I would have stayed over, but I knew we both had things to catch up on the next day. At first, I wondered if he was tired of me, but he grabbed me when the car was warming up and held me in his arms. He drove me home and wrote me a sweet text afterward: "Sweet dreams, cutie pie! I'm home safe! I had a great vacation with you! It was full of love, sunshine, laughter, and happiness!"

I heard from Greg only once the next day, and he met me at church on Sunday. Afterward, we had brunch and he came over to my condo. We went for a walk, and he stayed to watch some of our shows and relax before the work week began. Before leaving, he asked if he could take home the inversion table he had let me borrow. He grabbed it, along with his pillow, and I jokingly said, "You're taking everything! Are you trying to tell me something?"

He laughed and replied, "No, the inversion table isn't being used, and when I come over I use a couch pillow anyway." After he left, I began to cry, which turned into a straight-out bawl. I don't know what came over me or the reason behind it. All I knew was that something was up. I felt unsure about what he saw for our future and knew I needed to ask.

The next day I prayed about the deeper questions I needed to ask Greg, along with the need to experience peace with his answers. From my journal:

April 13, 2018

When will I ever listen to the pull on my heart? Through prayer and talking to my mom and a close friend I've known since the sixth grade, I had the courage and strength to bring up a conversation with Greg that has led to the peace I am feeling this morning.

Greg came over before his soccer game last night. As we were eating and talking, I expressed how difficult this week had been. I told him that I've been trying to figure out this gap or disconnect I've been feeling. I knew I had to express my feelings, even though I feared how the conversation might end. We didn't get into the deeper, heavier stuff because we had to leave for his soccer game.

However, when we got back we sat on the couch and spent about two hours talking.

Greg expressed that he needs time to heal in order to love, commit, and be all in the way he wants to be with me. We are on different "levels" in our relationship at the moment, and until he arrives at where I am, we aren't truly compatible. I love and care about him, and, although it's hard to admit, I have to fully give him the time he needs for the Lord to heal and grow his heart.

He has shown me so much in a relationship. No matter what might happen between us in the future, I know I am stronger and have learned so much along the way. I pray for his healing, for God to move the rocks weighing him down in order for him to blossom and grow.

We talked. He said he was sorry. I asked if we could pray together. Afterward, I told him that it was going to be hard to not text, call, talk to, or see him.

"You can always text me," he replied.

"No, I really can't. In order for you to heal properly, I just can't."

"I understand."

As we got up from the couch and walked to the door, Greg stopped to grab some of the food and drink he had brought over. We embraced. He gave me the longest hug and kissed me a couple of times. As he pulled away, he kissed my forehead, which had been one of my favorite gestures. I opened the door. We looked at each other as we said goodbye, and he left. A few seconds later . . . knock, knock, knock.

"I figure you probably want this back" (as he handed me the key I had given him to my condo).

"Thank you."

"Bye, Stace."

"Bye."

I went to my window, as I had done many times before. As I stood there watching him drive away, I felt an unexplainable peace and calmness reassuring me that everything was going to be okay.

I texted my friend Joe, knowing that he would be up at this hour since he was in a different time zone. I was able to reflect a little more with him before falling asleep and was thankful that he was up and, yet again, there for me.

The next morning I woke up to a text from a close friend:

Oh, Stacey! I am heartbroken for how you are feeling and how it went last night. I know that it took tremendous courage on your part taking that chance, to have it all end that way. I am really proud of you but really sad for you, too. I don't know what was said last night, and even if or when you choose to tell me I won't hate Greg. I especially don't hate him for last night because that was already something I had seen/felt, not something he suddenly did. I could tell from what you've shared with me that his heart wasn't invested nearly as deeply as yours in each other's lives and in God's calling for how to live your life. I'm not sure which of these worried me more for you.

Resentment can be a destroyer; the truth is, though, that when you hold resentment toward another person, the only person you're truly hurting is yourself. When you hold onto resentment, you hold it in your heart, which can be the most damaging choice you can make.

I don't think Greg is a bad person or even that it's about "Well, he did this . . . then he did that . . . ," naming all the mistakes he's made. We all make mistakes. It really comes down to his heart needing to grow. It needs to grow for God, so he can live a fuller life, which will then include being able to be a part of a relationship.

Despite everything that has happened, I still hope that might be with you. He says he needs time to heal, but I think he needs time to grow. I think he is a very kind person, easy to talk to, caring . . . but it's like you dig down below those things and there's a hard rock. A seed can't grow where the rocks are, on top of the nutrient-filled soil. Maybe it will take some work on his part to get those rocks out so he can plant something that will grow, blossom, and last.

If he is able to do so, this will produce great things. Until then, you two won't be truly compatible because *you already have* deep roots. You've been spending the past two years or so pulling out those last few rocks, and you're now ready for a healthy relationship to be planted (Matthew 13). I don't know if that will be with Greg, and I cannot say I will be sad if it isn't with him (which is the human, protective sister, friend side of me), *but*, if it is, I will celebrate with you! I will truly be happy because, if it comes full circle, it will mean that you guys will have an amazing story to tell of God's work in your lives.

Even though you probably feel defeated, this is a victory! You followed God's pull on your heart, and only good can come from that. We just don't know how long it will take to see it.

And with that, I knew the third and final round had officially become the knockout round. It was time to move forward.

When a breakup occurs after you've been together for quite a while, you have a choice. You can choose to stay stuck, or you can opt to move forward for your own sake, sanity, and growth. Resentment can be a destroyer; the truth is, though, that when you hold resentment toward another person, the only person you're truly hurting is yourself. When you hold onto resentment, you hold it in your heart, which can be the most damaging choice you can make. What do you do when your heart is broken? What do you do when you thought you were going to spend the rest of your life with this person and find out that may not be the reality? What do you do when your plans for the future seem shattered?

You make a choice.

You choose to remain on the floor with the shattered pieces around you, or you decide to slowly start gathering them up again. You pick them up one by one until you begin to hurt a little less, and you start rebuilding what you had thought was lost.

You cry.

You reflect.

You start looking within.

You take the time.

You listen to others' stories.

You delete the photos, text messages, and voicemails.

Over time, you remove all the things that remind you of what you had—or thought you had—with this person. In the process you grow, you rebuild, and you realize that life doesn't end when a breakup occurs. Remember that God sees if and when you're ready for what, or who, could be next.

Referring to this rebuilding time, a pastor once described a bell tower when speaking about love. If you're unfamiliar with a bell tower, think of a tower in a church building, holding at the top a bell of some sort. The bell is connected to a large rope that hangs the length of the tower, such that, when the rope is pulled, the bell rings. If you pull the rope just once and let go, the bell rings and continues to ring more and more softly until the reverberation stops. However, if you pull the rope, wait for a few seconds, and then grab it again, the bell will go back to the louder clanging. The reverberation then takes more time to grow softer, with the bell eventually settling into its resting spot and not making a sound.

When I heard this analogy, I connected it to my breakup with Greg four months earlier. This was a helpful analogy for me: I was still willing to let him figure things out, holding onto the rope but waiting to pull it again, knowing that it would clang more loudly if or when we reconnected. I realized that I had to stop pulling the rope in order for the clanging to dissipate and eventually stop, allowing me back into a peaceful state of being.

This. Is. Not. Easy! However, speaking from experience, it is worth it! I wish I could look you in the eye and tell you that this realization came overnight for me, but it didn't. It wasn't until three years later, when I was with a few friends, that the clanging finally stopped and I was able to move on fully, once and for all. And it wasn't until two years after that, when I unexpectedly crossed paths with Greg in the Atlanta airport, of all places, that this chapter in my life fully closed and I recognized how much I had grown.

According to many online surveys, it takes between three and six months to heal and move on from an ex. For me it was four months; however, although I moved on, I certainly wasn't healed.

PAUSE AND REFLECT

When you think about love,

- What are some things about it that you were never told?
- How has this realization affected your journey toward discovering love?

chapter 9

The Importance of Communication

ONE FALL WEEKEND a bunch of friends were in town for a college golf outing. We planned to meet up for a night out afterward. While dating Greg, I had felt as though I had become less worried about an on-time arrival, but my excitement to see everyone motivated me to get to the bar early that night. I put in my name and glanced at the bar to see if there were any empty seats so I could grab a drink before everyone else arrived. There were two seats, one on one side of the bar and one on the other, next to a cute guy!

I chose the latter.

As I ordered a drink and sat there, I couldn't help but overhear the conversation this guy was having with his friend, who was sitting next to him. I had the urge to join the conversation—so I did! We started chatting, and then the buzzer went off, signaling that my table was ready. I left them but assured them that I would be back.

My friends arrived, but in the back of my mind I kept thinking, *I hope those guys didn't leave. How do I get back in there?* One of my college roommates (remember Kennedy?) was on her way, and I excused myself to use the restroom before she got there. I noticed that the guys were still at the bar, so when I was finished I walked back over there. While I was talking to them, Kennedy arrived. I introduced her and invited them to join us if they felt like it. Kennedy and I left to go back outside, which gave me time to catch her up on what had happened prior to her arrival.

A little while later, Jay and Jake walked out the door to join us. One of them had initially caught my eye more than the other, but as we got to talking I found that the other was more interesting to me. So, when he sat down next to me, I felt a rush of excitement.

As the night went on, the drinks and laughter continued. However, someone had once told me that nothing good ever happens after midnight. (Not going to lie, I wish I'd heard this while I was in college!) I put in for an Uber and said goodbye to my friends, and Jay walked me out. While we were waiting for the Uber, he asked for my number, which I, of course, gave him. We hugged, and I jumped into the Uber, hoping he would call! If nothing else, this had been an unexpectedly fun night out with friends, an opportunity to meet new people, and a chance to put myself back out there again.

The next day, while I was out running errands, I scrolled down in my texts and noticed an unknown number. I didn't know how I had missed it or if it hadn't come through right away, but it was Jay! He said that our meeting had been unexpected and that he'd had a lot of fun. He also asked if I'd be interested in going out soon.

Uh, yeah! In the meantime, though, I would be meeting up with friends downtown for another night out. This occasion was different from the previous one . . . drinks, shots, nonstop laughter, and a lot of dancing! It brought me back to our college days and reminded me how much I had missed that particular group of friends!

Before leaving, one of my friends pulled me in for a hug and said, "Stace, the guys and I were talking earlier about how much more confident you are now than ever before. I want you to know that your man is out there!" We hugged and said our goodbyes. As I Ubered home, I felt the tears welling. I truly felt that I was exactly where I was supposed to be, surrounded by friends who had known me for years and were able to notice my transformation. Little did I know that I was just getting started!

Wait for It . . .

You never know what to expect on a first date. The one thing I had going for me this time, compared to prior online dating experiences, was that I had already spent a few hours with Jay, getting to know him a little. We decided to go out that next Friday. So, during the week I did what I do best when starting to talk to a guy: I Google stalk. With all I had gone through with Scammer, I learned to start investigating earlier on with any new man I might end up spending time with. One thing I found out was that Jay had once been married. He looked very young in the wedding photos that were online, and I told myself not to jump to any conclusions. Everyone has a story, and I was looking forward to hearing his.

Friday arrived, and I was nervous. Our night consisted of having drinks and an appetizer at a bar before going to a comedy show downtown. Since we didn't get dinner before the show, we walked to a favorite Mexican spot afterward. Jay and I got a round of margaritas and some chips and guac. I remember thinking to myself, *He hasn't brought up being married yet. How do I get him to share this part of his history with me because I cannot leave this night not knowing*!

I shared parts of my story about Scammer in the hope of his becoming more comfortable sharing his. Eventually, he did! I could tell right away that he felt embarrassed about his divorce and that it was something he certainly wasn't proud of, especially having been raised in a Christian household, having gone to a Christian school, etc. I leaned in, listened, and reassured him that we all have a past. We all have a story worth sharing. One that has shaped us to be the people we are today. I thanked him for sharing his and for being vulnerable. Inside, I was sighing with relief and feeling an even deeper appreciation of and attraction to him. I respect him for trusting me enough on that first date to share some of it.

I have a few thoughts about my own generation regarding relationships, marriage, and divorce. I always had my "plans" to graduate college, get married by 25, and have children shortly thereafter. *Ha!* I look back now and think, *Why would I have wanted that*? Twenty-five is so young. At that age I was just starting to discover who I was as a person, and it has taken me the past ten plus years to see myself as the beautiful soul I now know I am! I feel that so many people view marriage as the "next thing" to do, according to some unwritten formula. This timetable has been instilled in us by society.

Of course, there are many couples who do marry young and grow together—which is something to be recognized and celebrated! However, there are also many couples who report that they have grown apart and are not who they once were, or who feel that their spouse isn't who they once were and that they need to part ways.

Any relationship takes work. Marriage takes work. You don't just get married and have children and know that all will be well. I have observed so many of my friends through the ups and downs of their marriages and applauded their determination to fight through, but I realize that none of this is easy. I truly believe that God will put the right person in my life when the timing is right. That's according to His time, not my time.

I also know that there are others who have found love again after divorce because they took the time to find out who they were before jumping into another relationship right away. Jay told me that this was what he did after his divorce. He also told me that he didn't talk to his ex-wife at all anymore, which was something I needed to hear because I knew that exes were a trigger for me from my last relationship with Greg.

After our leaving the Mexican restaurant that night, Jay drove me home and walked me to my door. I invited him in, and he immediately started making out with me. I realize that we had both been drinking, but I remember feeling in that moment that I shouldn't have let him in. His kissing was pretty forceful, and I was taken a little aback.

I ended up telling him that he needed to leave because I knew I wanted to protect myself from any type of sexual relationship right then; knowing this would be a topic of conversation in the future if we were to end up dating. He had been nothing but respectful the whole night—opening doors and paying for everything, and he even texted me when he arrived home safely. I was definitely open to seeing him again, and, as far as first dates go, it had been a good one!

When you think about dating, what comes to mind? Giddiness? Excitement? Anxiety? Frustration? Exhaustion? Hope? There are different seasons pertaining to dating and relationships and you feel all the different feelings in each. The season I was in was dating in hopes of it leading to marriage. I don't know about you, but I always have some hesitation when starting a dating relationship. This can be the result of what we have endured from our past relationships and traumas.

I believe that hesitation is your body protecting itself from putting it out there again, knowing that there is always a possibility you will get hurt. This feeling came a couple weeks into dating Jay. We went to the Farmer's Market and then back to his place to cook lunch. While we were cooking and eating, I felt my nerves surfacing and my gut kicking in. After we ate, we relaxed by the pool and had a deep conversation, during which I opened my heart more about my past.

When I got home, I found myself crying, thanks to all the emotions and feelings I had been holding in all day. Everything seemed to be going perfectly, but I wondered how things could be falling into place like this. Jay seemed to "check off" all the qualities I want in a man/husband, so why was I feeling uneasy? Was it because I'd been hurt in the past? Was it because I thought I had "found the one," and it had ended in heartbreak?

Maybe the difference was that I wasn't the one "looking to find" this time and that I was letting God take control. Love is about opening up to someone wholeheartedly and risking it all. I felt hopeful that I wouldn't get hurt again, but I didn't know. I had to trust that God had this relationship in His hands as I prayed for stillness, patience, and peace.

The next day Jay and I became "official." What does that mean, exactly? According to a couple of different sources: "if a piece of information is official, it has been announced publicly with authority" (Cambridge English Dictionary) and "one who holds and is invested" (Merriam-Webster).

A commitment. An investment.

Both take time, energy, money, and heart.

Both involve taking a risk.

Both can rock your world in unexpected ways.

Both can create memories.

Both can break you.

Both can open opportunities that you might never have experienced before.

This time was challenging for me. I was trying to open my heart again, but my mind kept drifting back to Greg. Then I would beat myself up and didn't understand why I still had him on my mind.

Why was I experiencing these feelings?

Why did I have to overthink everything, encouraging anxiety, wondering, and worry when I wanted it all to disappear so I could enjoy this newly blossoming relationship?

Was my gut trying to speak to me again, and I wasn't listening?

Did my mind take over my heart or my heart take over my mind, trying to tell one another opposite stories until my mind got entangled in the lies I had experienced three years earlier with Scammer and the distrust that had shattered me with Greg?

Yes—to it all!

These feelings were real.

These feelings were driven by the fear of getting hurt yet again.

These feelings were trying to protect me.

Learning to truly sit with these feelings, thoughts, and doubts is challenging, but sitting with feelings is essential. I felt multiple times that I was trying to sabotage the goodness that Jay was bringing into my life. I felt that I wasn't allowing myself to let go of being hurt in the past in order to embrace what was in front of me. However, I now recognize it all as part of the process of growing in love—love not just for another but love for myself.

Twenty-six days later Jay told me he was falling in love with me! I wept in his arms, trying to explain what was going on in my mind. He was comforting me and expressing that it was a little terrifying for him, too, knowing it had been only three weeks. He shared with me that he hadn't ever felt this way so early in a relationship. I didn't know what to do, what to say, what to think, or how to feel! I've asked this before, but how do you know when you're falling in love with someone? I've been told that you "just do," but this time it was unexpected, and I didn't allow myself to get to the core of it all.

Looking back, I can say that I was still grieving the loss of a relationship, trying to figure out how to balance everything in my life, beginning a new relationship that my innocent soul wanted so badly to work, and feeling that God had put this man into my life for a reason. I didn't respond to Jay's "I love you" that night because I knew I needed more time. I found myself pausing. Pausing is important because we live in a culture of instant gratification. People aren't used to the pause. It's okay to wait, to take the time to really assess the situation and think about how you will respond, especially when feelings are involved.

Pausing is important because we live in a culture of instant gratification. People aren't used to the pause. It's okay to wait, to take the time to really assess the situation and think about how you will respond, especially when feelings are involved.

Four months into our relationship, we were talking rings. I kept asking myself, *How will I know*? I was trying to sort this all out, my mind was in overdrive, and I was searching for clarity. Due to the circumstances of my past, I was constantly asking myself how I could have been the only one Jay was interested in.

I had gone through almost seven years of talking to Scammer—nearly seven years of his telling me I wasn't enough and me fighting for his attention, fighting to be "the one" he would choose. Then I had been with Greg for two years, during which, once again, I had felt as though I wasn't enough because his ex kept trying to get back into his life. With Jay, I was the only one he was interested in, and because of all I'd been through that was scary to comprehend. How could someone be fully interested in *me* when I had felt broken for so long?

This is what abuse can do to someone. Emotional, mental, and/or physical abuse all change the wiring of your brain. Unless you're ready to see this, accept it, and do the work to start the unwiring and rewiring process, you will never truly know what life could be like. The one thing I know and continue to remind myself of is that none of this had been my fault. Bad things happen to good people. It's the people you surround yourself with afterward that make a world of difference.

Jay and I talked about where we saw ourselves in one year and then in five years. I brought up the concept of being "all in," and we had continued conversations about engagement and even having children. I was still feeling a little apprehensive but was trying hard to give myself the grace and mercy to trust God. And then came December 19, 2018.

It was our last week of school before the holiday break. I hadn't been feeling well all week. As with any other morning, I woke up and started reading my devotional and writing in my journal. But shortly afterward I found myself in the bathroom throwing up. I hardly ever call in sick, but that was obviously what I had to do that day.

After quickly writing up substitute lesson plans, I crawled back into bed to sleep a little more. While I was sleeping, I heard my doorbell ring, but I hardly had the energy to get up. When I did, I opened the door and saw that my mail was rubber banded on top of a box. I knew the package was my Christmas gift for my family, but what I wasn't expecting was what I saw when I turned over the pile of mail. The envelope on top of the stack was addressed to me with a handwriting I knew. It was from Greg! I was shocked and unsure what to do.

I started shaking as I sat down on my couch and stared at the envelope. I texted Michelle. I just didn't understand! Why, after seven months (there's that number again), did Greg decide to write this letter to me when I was now with Jay? Michelle suggested that I practice adulting by not opening it and instead sending it back. In my heart I knew I couldn't do that. Part of me was hoping this would bring the ultimate closure I needed.

When I was ready, I opened it, read it, cried, and processed the message. It was a three-page, handwritten letter expressing sentiments similar to what Greg had said to me before. After I had finished reading it, I asked God to give me the strength to continue to move forward with the man He had put into my life. Communication is essential, so I ended up sharing with Jay that I had received this letter. I told him that he was more than welcome to read it because I didn't want anything to come between us. He respectfully told me that he would rather not because Greg had written those words for me. As I began to tear it up, I realized that I had received this letter on Greg's 39th birthday.

Greg had mailed me a letter to communicate his feelings, but there are many other forms of communication we use as well: text, phone call, email, Instagram, Facebook, Twitter, and whatever else is out there that distracts us from what so many relationships lack—an authentic, sit-across-from-each-other or side-by-side on the couch kind of conversation. This type of communication brings an intimacy and safety that no form of technology can replace. Through my years of counseling and sessions with my life coach, I have learned that communicating and sharing what is on your heart, mind, and soul might be scary at first but is always worth it in the end.

Sharing past experiences with your significant other is necessary for you to heal and grow together. Jay and I committed to not having sex until marriage. Was it easy? Nope. Did we do other things? Yes. Was it probably harder for Jay than for me? I believe so, since I desire emotional intimacy before sexual intimacy enters the picture—which is so countercultural. This was my first relationship in which I had set that boundary from the beginning. Once you have sex, it tends to cloud your thoughts and introduces another level into your relationship—one that tends to stifle other aspects of getting to know each other on a deeper level emotionally, mentally, and spiritually.

Jay and I read some books together as a couple, which opened us up to deeper conversation. However, as time went on, I started to reflect and recognized that I was the one who seemed to be bringing up harder conversations and asking about past relationships or experiences, eager to learn more about the person I thought I was in love with. I felt as though I was sharing my heart and what was on my mind but never getting the same in return.

Obviously, men and women tend to communicate on different levels. However, when you have a face-to-face conversation rather than texting or messaging, it brings another level to the dialogue, since each person is able to witness the other's nonverbal cues while they are sharing.

This isn't easy. Communication is something you need to work on daily. Communication opens you up to what can for some be a make-or-break vulnerability. I find that people tend to hold things in, walking around pretending that life is just how they have envisioned it to be—to put their heads down, engage primarily with their phones, and block out the real-life people right in front of them. But if you truly look into a person's eyes and ask, "How are you *really* doing?" you had better be ready for a conversation that could reveal a side of them you might not have seen before.

Creating a safe environment for these conversations is the first step for people to be authentic, genuine, and vulnerable. This is what I prayed and hoped for with Jay. I started to slowly recognize, though, that this kind of openness might not have been one of his strengths. I was also discovering that this kind of mutual sharing was something I needed in a relationship.

Friendships and romantic relationships aren't guaranteed to last forever, but the ones in which you invest your time and energy have a higher chance of thriving at a deeper level. Throughout my life I have experienced loss in both friendships and relationships. I might not always know the reasons why, or whether the issue is just that time has separated us, but I do know that God had put each of my earlier relationships in my life for a reason—to help me show up and find myself along the way. As I continue to hold onto this thinking and am guided by God to move forward, I pray for all the friendships and relationships that no longer are. Instead of feeling sad, hurt, and uncertain, I want to remember that each one of them has taught me something along the way in this journey we call life.

PAUSE AND REFLECT

- In what ways are you able to relate to this?
- Does this bring to the surface any emotions or any people in your life you were once close with?

I continued to try to communicate with Jay openly and honestly. We spent part of our first summer together hiking at Pictured Rocks National Lakeshore in Michigan's Upper Peninsula. I will always remember walking behind him, fully present in God's natural beauty and thinking to myself, *This is it! He is the one I can see myself doing life with, hiking to different places, getting lost together, and laughing the days and nights away with each other.* This is why we date: to continue to see people evolve and develop over time. I felt this way in that moment when away from our everyday lives, but after returning home I found myself continuing to want to control the situation.

At the time I was reading a book by Holley Gerth titled *You're Already Amazing*. One of the chapters was about control. As women, we feel as though we have to show a certain amount of control to protect ourselves from getting hurt. We want to remain safe. However, the emotion that brings out this feeling for control is fear. Ensuring that we will be safe equates in our minds to knowing in advance what is going to happen—which, in an endless circle, seems to necessitate our being in charge and in control of it all.

I know that this is something I struggle with and that I must give over this tendency to God daily. He is the only One I want to have in control of my life, so that I can feel not only safe but *secure*! I love Holley Gerth's repeated refrain, "Life is a risk. Love is a risk." This author goes on to offer a quote from C. S. Lewis: "To love at all is to be vulnerable. Love anything, and your heart will certainly be wrung and possibly broken."

Lewis mentions that, if we want to keep love intact and safe, we need to bury ourselves, to wrap our hearts around things we can control, so as to not get hurt. If we do not love, our heart "will not be broken; it will become unbreakable, impenetrable, and irredeemable." I don't know about you, but this is not the kind of love I want! I commit to the risk of being open to whatever love and life will bring me. I know that all I need will be provided for me because of my faith, hope, and love.

Jay and I went shopping for rings, continuing to talk more seriously about marriage and even about raising kids someday. Our one-year anniversary was approaching, and, in anticipation of what might happen, I did what any woman who feels herself to be in love might do . . . I got my nails done! Jay made the day special by taking me out to breakfast, doing a ropes course together, and then going out to dinner. I would be lying if I said my heart wasn't a little bit deflated when the night ended and there was no ring. Although this was hard for me to accept, my hope was in knowing that God had a plan, even though it might not be precisely the one I envisioned.

In August, my friend Bridget posted on her social media a photograph of herself and her husband with the following caption:

> Of all the gin joints in all the towns in all the world, he walked into mine. 25 years ago today, we walked into our yard to the strains of Handel and vowed to help each other become better humans. To belly laugh and ugly cry. To forgive, strengthen, accept, sustain. And each day we try.

I couldn't stop thinking about the words she had posted. I knew this was how I wanted my marriage someday to be and to feel. Through the good times and the trying times. Through the hurt and the joy. Through the laughs, smiles, and tears. A partnership. A team. Not me against him or him against me. Each of us a person to come alongside the other, to remind one another of the faith, hope, love, and trust we hold together in God. Whenever life puts two human beings together, there will be problems and issues that arise. It's *how* you communicate and navigate these times together that will not only grow your marriage but make it thrive!

Timothy Keller says in *The Meaning of Marriage*, "If two spouses each say, 'I'm going to treat my self-centeredness as the main problem in the marriage,' you have the prospect of a truly great marriage." You could change *spouses* to *significant others* and *marriage* to *relationship* in this sentence, and the dynamic will still work. Either way, self-centeredness is inevitable. Why? Because we are all human. We are broken. Eve took and ate from the tree of forbidden fruit in the Garden of Eden. Adam stood there saying nothing and then chose to eat the fruit himself. We are each full of self-centered pride, greed, envy, and lust, which are among the seven deadly sins described in the Bible. Self-centeredness is a broken human trait we all possess.

I loved learning about the development of a child from birth to the age of seven when I was getting my master's degree in Early Childhood Development. Toddlers and young children are egocentric. Life is all about them. They thrive on attention. They go through separation anxiety. They want to play when they want to play, and they don't care who they steal from because they don't know any better . . . yet. Until they have guidance, are taught, and have behavior modeled for them, they expect things to go their way. We all know that this is not life.

However, despite the endless modeling and learning, we all fail. We just do—again because we are human. For most of my life, I internalized failing as a bad thing. But I have learned that failure is the way we grow. Failure is something we all need to embrace—and not just when we're young. The knowledge and acceptance that we will fail in our jobs, our relationships, and our lives needs to be normalized. There is no perfection here on this earth, and there never will be until our Savior comes again. What we can do in the meantime is talk about our failures and mistakes, own them, grow from them, and offer grace to ourselves and to others who fail us along the way.

As 2019 wound down, I began to feel the pressure the world tends to put on you after you have dated someone for a while. I wanted to quiet the noise that seemed to be coming from everyone by shouting, "I don't know what to tell you! I don't know why there hasn't been a proposal yet!" I believed in my heart that this just wasn't the right time, but this was also the time when I was becoming more aware of the lack of meaningful communication with Jay.

This problem continued even after our having conversations about how it worried me when he didn't text in a timely manner or how I created stories in my mind about why he didn't. I came to realize that feeling these things stemmed from my earlier trauma with Scammer and Greg. The story I was telling myself was, *He must not care about me. He's probably talking to another girl. I know that he checks Facebook periodically, so how hard would it be to shoot me a text to say hi and ask how I'm doing*? These thoughts, detrimental as they were, were real.

Some of you might need to hear or be reminded of this: Don't ever think there is something wrong with you! Your thoughts, feelings, and emotions are all valid. Although we get entangled in our own thoughts far more often than we want to, we need to talk about our misgivings, regardless of how "silly" they may sound.

I recognized that I was still healing from the hurt I had experienced from Greg and knew that this probably wasn't fair to Jay. Even though I was working through this healing, I was sharing it all openly with Jay. I wasn't sure, however, that he was ready to fully open his heart and let me in, which was hard to admit.

Fast forward five months, and the world shut down due to the COVID-19 pandemic. Jay left to spend time with his sister and her family. I was happy he was able to get away but was quickly hit again with insecurity due to his lack of communication. Jay didn't text very often or call at all. He told me one night that they were having a bonfire with some of his sister's friends, and my mind went into overdrive. *What friends? Are any of them single women? Should I be worried?*

Sometimes helping is just being there, not saying a word.

The questioning, the overthinking, the narratives I constantly told myself were all rooted in past relationships and the insecurity that had surfaced from them. Will I ever fully grieve and heal from these insecurities? Probably not, but I am more aware of them and their role in my thought processes than I used to be and remind myself regularly that they are a part of my story. I wanted to counteract the negative thoughts and narratives as I reminded myself that Jay was not Scammer. He was not Greg. He was Jay, and he had done nothing to make me think he couldn't be trusted.

In times of sadness, heaviness, loneliness, and loss people want you to listen and be there. They don't necessarily want you to talk, offer advice, or assure them that everything will be okay. We must remember to allow space for acceptance and healing to happen for others, even though we might want to help fix the problem and make our loved ones, or ourselves, smile again. Sometimes helping is just being there, not saying a word.

On a scale of 1–10 (1 being not important at all, 10 being essential), how important is communication to you within a relationship?

- What does it mean to communicate?
- How effective are you as a communicator?
- What do you look for in others in terms of communication?

chapter 10

The End Is Near

I USED TO LOVE roller coasters: the anticipation as the cars slowly—*click*, *click*, *click*—make their way up the hill just before getting to the top, followed by the *whoosh* . . . the thrill, the drop in your stomach on the way down, screaming, laughing, holding on for dear life, praying and hoping the bar on your lap holding you in stays put! The anticipation seemed to take so much longer than the ride back to home base. As I got older, though, I started to realize that my love for roller coasters was dwindling. It became apparent that it felt safer for me to be back at home base, where my head wasn't being jostled around.

Before heading to Hocking Hills, Ohio, with Jay for our summer adventure, I was telling people that I felt as though I were on a roller coaster of emotions, mentally and physically—and I wanted off! My gut was hitting me strongly; let me remind you that it speaks to me in this way, usually meaning that something is about to happen. Something just didn't feel right. I felt anxiety start creeping in as Jay and I hopped in the car at the end of July 2020 to drive to Hocking Hills.

When we got there, we found a cute little outdoor winery with a live band. While enjoying the live music and our wine flights, Jay asked me, if there was one thing I could change about myself, what it would be. I told him that, although I know God has made me to be the person I am, I could let go of having such a strong inner critic and overthinking things constantly. Jay then shared that he would change his lack of discipline, along with becoming more extroverted. I found it interesting that he talked about his lack of discipline, but actions on his part to change that deficit never seemed to happen.

The next couple of days we hiked all around Hocking Hills, exploring nature and embracing all the natural beauty, such as the waterfalls, caves, and paths. On our last night there, we grabbed a pizza and came back to sit on the little balcony at our bed and breakfast while we enjoyed some wine. We ended up getting into yet another disagreement, this one about public versus charter schools. I became upset and finally said I was done talking about this issue.

I went inside, got ready for bed, and lay down on my side, holding back tears and hoping that Jay would cross the barrier that seemed to be dividing us and that he would hold me. This didn't happen. Instead, my brain was racing. *Does he still love me? Is he going to break up with me? Will/Does he support me as a public-school educator?* My inner critic was running nonstop, replaying the conversation.

We woke up the next morning, ate breakfast, and packed the car to start our six-hour drive home. Something still felt off. When spending an extended amount of time together, one of the things we had jokingly asked one another on previous trips was whether one of us was tired of the other. I remember turning a corner very early in our drive and asking in a joking tone, as we usually did, "So, are you tired of me yet?" He gave me a little smile and said, "No." I responded with a giggle, "Well, I guess I'll really know the truth if you end up breaking up with me in a few days!" (I don't recommend responding like this.)

I parked in the roundabout to his condo. He gave me a kiss, got out, opened the door to get one of his bags, and then went to the trunk to retrieve his suitcase. I looked in the rearview mirror as he was pulling out his suitcase, my gut in a twisted knot. I turned around just before he shut the trunk door and said, "Okay. Well, I love you!" He said it back, but not in his usual tone. He shut the door and started walking up the stairs to the entrance of his condo. I sat there thinking, praying, and wondering. As tears started to well, I began the drive home; knowing that something was not right but hoping my gut's alarm was invalid. (Had it ever been wrong before? Nope!)

Thirty-eight hours later and I still hadn't heard anything from Jay. I didn't know what to do or think and prayed for understanding: "Lord, You are the only One who will always be by my side. You are the only One who will never let me down. You are the only One about whom I never have to wonder where You are!"

The next day I watched Jay walk into my condo and I could tell by his body language that he had something to tell me. As the key I had given him turned in the lock, I got up from the couch and walked into my kitchen from one direction as he came in through the other.

Our eyes met, and I knew. He pulled me in for a hug as he said, "Stace, we need to talk." I gently pulled away and admitted, "I have felt that something has been off."

"So, we are getting to the two-year mark, and we have always said that we are dating to either get married or . . . *(his voice trailed off)* part ways." With tears starting to well in his eyes, he continued, "I think it's best if we part ways."

Although I had known it deep down (because, let's face it, it was the same gut feeling I'd had when Greg came over to tell me he needed to figure things out with his ex before moving forward with me), it still sucked. I don't remember whether I burst into tears, led Jay to the couch for him to tell me more, or what exactly happened next. It was all kind of a blur. What I do remember is his telling me that he had gone back into gaming and was engaging in an addiction he'd had prior to meeting me and that he had been ashamed to tell me. He shared with me that he had looked for rings five or six times but that something was holding him back. He had met up with his mom the day before and told her. She had responded that, if he didn't see a future with me, it was certainly not fair to string me along.

By this time I was in tears, so I excused myself to the bathroom and tried to catch my breath. We continued to talk, and he kept reciting to me the classic statement I hear all the time: "You are such an amazing woman. It's not you, it's me." I listened. I cried. I encouraged him to get outside help for his addiction. We prayed for one another before he gave me one last hug and left my condo for the last time. I went to the window with tears streaming down my face as he looked up and we waved goodbye, as we usually did.

I texted three of my closest friends right away, followed by my mom. Two of them rushed right over, wine in hand, to listen, comfort, and support me. Both helped me see that Jay was not in a healthy state and that he needed to get better before he committed to anything. Hearing this reminded me that I didn't want to start a marriage with someone who wasn't his healthiest self. I felt incredibly grateful that two of my friends had been willing to drop everything to be by my side that evening.

I cried some more after they left, took a hot shower and climbed into bed. I knew that I was going to be more than okay as a comforting and peaceful feeling covered me up like a warm blanket as I fell asleep praying.

The next day I woke up and slowly started my quiet time. When it came time for my journaling, I wrote directly to God, brain dumping out all my questions. I was wondering so many things and reminding myself that He wants to hear it all! My journaling from that morning reflects my state of mind:

> I am heartbroken, sad, and confused, and I just don't understand. There was a reason I felt "off"—I knew something was going on. There's a reason my gut was speaking to me yet again. Although I have this peaceful feeling, it still doesn't take away from the fact that being in this space sucks. *Have I known this for a while? Did I always have the feeling that I needed to guard my heart?* This has happened many times. I just don't understand, God! I'm trying to be strong, but *why does this happen to me? Do guys just realize when dating me how strong I am and that they have work to do on themselves after being with me?*
>
> I just want a man who is healthy enough to commit to and be fully in with me, so I don't have to worry about his ever leaving! *Will that ever happen? Am I meant to be alone for the rest of my life?*

I know I'm not really alone because I have You always by my side. You have also brought me my family and friends. I just feel ready, though, to find my person, my best friend, my partner to do life with here on this earth and to create a family with. Sometimes I wish I had a Magic 8 Ball to show me if this is in my plan. I know, I know—trust!

> Trust You!
> Trust the process.
> Trust myself.
> Please, Lord, just as I want healing for Jay,
> please work on me and heal my heart.
>
> "Be still and know that I am God." Psalm 46:10 (NIV)
> Be still and know that I am
> Be still and know that I
> Be still and know
> Be still and
> Be still
> Be
> . . . just BE! ❤

Della Hicks-Wilson posted once on Instagram, "Darling, you feel heavy because you are too full of truth. Open your mouth more. Let the truth exist somewhere other than inside your body."

Brain dumps can happen anywhere and at any time. All you need is paper and pen or a computer. Pick up that pen and just dump out everything you've been holding in. Write it all down on paper or in a document on your computer. Type it in a text to a close friend. Be honest with yourself and don't hold anything back. A brain dump puts your thoughts and feelings all in one place so you don't have to keep them in your mind, which often wreaks havoc. Brain dumps don't always solve the problem, but they can help. I like to say that what we hold inside is always better out than in. Brain dumps help you continue through the grieving process rather than being stuck in it.

Della Hicks-Wilson posted once on Instagram, "Darling, you feel heavy because you are too full of truth. Open your mouth more. Let the truth exist somewhere other than inside your body."

Your thoughts matter. Your feelings matter. Your words matter. Let them flow freely for others to hear and help. In return, you will continue to heal. God is there no matter when you need Him. Pick up the pen or, better yet, just start talking. He is listening!

Shortly after what would have been my second anniversary with Jay, I wrote the following to lay out the desires of my heart before God:

> *Lord, I pray that You have a man for me who has and shows love for You every day, digging deeply into Your Word and following You.*
>
> » *One who balances me out and vice versa.*
> » *One who is motivated, disciplined, eager to try new things, takes adventures, and pushes me—mind, body, and soul.*
> » *One who has done the work to become the best version of himself, one who has the desire to continue to grow as a person, along with supporting me in my growth.*
> » *One who communicates and values open and honest conversations.*
> » *One who is financially stable, lives on his own, and is ready to invest in a relationship, a marriage, and someday fatherhood.*
> » *One who is confident in himself but humble, knowing that his identity in You is greater than anything else and is all he needs.*
> » *One who can grow in faith and with whom our foundation is apparent as we live to show Your love, understand our selfishness, and know that neither of us is perfect.*
> » *One who will wait to have sex until marriage in order to build our relationship on a spiritual and emotional level first.*

- *One who loves life to the fullest!*
- *One who takes time every day to spend with You.*
- *One who is successful and has a genuine desire to be with me and loves me as unconditionally as is humanly possible.*
- *One who makes me belly laugh.*
- *One who is active and enjoys being outdoors in Your beauty.*
- *One who accepts me fully—past, present, and future—and I him!*

I know that might be detailed and in depth, but You know the desires of my heart, Lord. I pray that, when this man is put into my life, You, above anyone else, will show me that he is the one You have chosen for me all along. Thank You, Lord, and I pray to live as Your obedient servant every day.

I've shared before about making lists of what we want in a significant other, but this prayer was different. It felt more complete.

The next day I met up with my friends from my small group. We walked around downtown and had dinner. Afterward, one of them walked with me to our cars. She looked at me and said, "Stace, I feel that, if this was the love of your life, you wouldn't be here right now but instead rolled up in a ball on the floor." This made me think, *Is she right? How will I ever know if I'll have a "love of my life?" Do I even believe there is a person out there to fulfill that?*

The only true love of my life is the Lord. He is always there, loving me unconditionally, wrapping me in His loving, gentle, forgiving, and hopeful arms. I read in one of the *Jesus Calling* devotional books, "Rest snuggly in My everlasting arms." That imagery is so beautiful to imagine. No matter what we go through. No matter what has happened in our lives. No matter where we might be going, One Person is always right there. At this moment in my life, I once again needed the tools, time, and space to heal in order to move forward and even find love again.

When I got home that night, I had the feeling that I needed to set up a time with Jay to get some of my stuff back. I texted Michelle, and she encouraged me to do it sooner rather than later—and without emotion. I thought, *Ha! Does she even know me?* I knew what she meant, though, and was determined to do just that . . . and to allow myself to cry afterward if I needed to.

I texted Jay, and immediately after pushing *Send*, I started crying. Spending two years with someone, along with all the memories, laughter, and conversations that go with it, leaves you with a lot to let go of in a short time (in this case, a week). However, I knew I needed to do this in order to continue to move forward and heal.

Three days later, there was still no response.

Well, this just made me annoyed and frustrated! The narrative I was telling myself was, *I guess two years together didn't mean anything to him!* One night shortly after this, I logged back into Instagram. I knew I needed to set boundaries, which then led to my making the decision to unfollow Jay and his whole family. (When you do this, did you know that you also need to click a button to make sure the other person is no longer following you?)

Although I unfollowed all of them, I still found, months later, photos popping up on my phone that seemed to be hidden in a secret iPhone land! I knew I would have photos of our past because of the Chatbooks I had printed out. However, I decided this was okay. It's important to be reminded that relationships are a part of our story. We end up growing from each one of them.

Jay eventually got back to me with a day and a time he would be able to meet up. I prayed all day. I had that feeling in my stomach that was just sloshing around, but I also had a support team that was there for me all day, encouraging me every step of the way! As I drove to where we had planned on meeting, songs played on the radio that I felt had been chosen just for me to calm my nerves and signal that everything was going to be okay.

I arrived early and headed to the stairs that overlooked the river. The sky was beautiful, the sun was about to set, and the wind was blowing, which I felt was the Holy Spirit reminding me that I was surrounded by love, courage, and grace! I prayed for the right words to say. I honestly didn't know what words and sentences would escape my mouth. What I did know was that, through prayer, I trusted that

God would provide the words I needed . . . which He most certainly did. I don't even recall what I said, but I do know that my words were delivered in a poised manner; that I spoke courageously and without emotion; and that, when I climbed back into my car, I felt free to move forward!

As I reflected on my way home, I felt that Jay was still confused and didn't know his purpose in life. We all need to be reminded that it isn't our job to "fix" anyone. The only one who can make any change is that person. In that moment I chose to acknowledge the grief that would inevitably still come from the loss of another relationship, but I also chose to realize that my relationship with Jay was yet another part of my ongoing story. I wasn't angry, but the loss I was feeling I knew to be a gift I would recognize over time. In the present moment, though, I knew I needed to allow myself the time to process, grieve, and heal—to not just move forward but to move on!

I asked the questions. I wanted the signs. I journaled. I prayed. I wanted to know why!

> *Lord,*
> *Why?*
> *Why am I still single?*
> *Why have you not brought into my life yet the man I will live this life with?*
> *Am I going to be able to enjoy marriage, as You intend for it to be enjoyed someday?*
> *Will I get to experience the sexual intimacy You have designed for a love only You can bring about, bonding a man and a woman so that we'll be shamelessly one in You?*
> *Will I get to experience having a child of my own to love and cherish, as You love and cherish all Your children?*
> *One I can raise in Your Name, for You?*
> *Why?*
> *Why am I still single?*
>
> *I know. I believe. I have faith in Your timing. But it's not easy. It's a challenge to see little ones with their parents surrounding me. It's not jealousy because I am so happy*

> *they get to experience that season, but I would like to know if that is in my future.*
>
> *You are the One I want to follow and trust, and I believe that You will provide for me. You know I'm sad about this, but expressing it out loud, in words, will hopefully help me to keep giving it to You.*

During this time, Philippians 4:6 (NIV) kept ringing in my ears: "Do not be anxious about anything." I shed many tears, and I'll bet you have, too. It's important to allow yourself to cry. Tears are not meant to be restrained or dammed up. They stream down your cheeks for a reason. When you dam them up, the floodgates will eventually open anyway, so letting them out when they're ready to flow is something we all need to embrace. As I've mentioned before, tears are meant to cleanse and to draw out the sadness, grief, and hurt, . . . and even joy and happiness!

The grief of a broken heart takes time to mend. Just as I had done when Greg and I broke things off, there came a night when I was looking through photos of myself and Jay. I began crying and asking more questions.

Why? We always had a wonderful time together, laughing, talking, and adventuring.

Do I miss him?

Do I miss having someone to hang out and have adventures with?

Do I miss that companionship?

I honestly didn't know the answer to any of these questions, but I did know that it was okay to ask them and grieve the loss of a friend. To grieve the loss of what I had thought we were going to experience next in our relationship. To grieve the loss of our relationship itself. To grieve, period. It's a process. It takes time. It takes faith. It takes hope, knowing there's a reason for it all. Often, we don't know what that reason is . . . yet.

I knew that God was about to bring many pieces of my puzzle together, and I was open to every one of them being sorted out and set into place. Most of all, I looked forward to someday seeing the bigger picture. I was tired of trying to be the one attempting to control every situation. I knew in my heart that He would guide my path, and I wanted to fully let go and trust Him.

For the remainder of 2020, I . . .

» Experienced a free energy clearing a friend had encouraged me to get.
» Wrote a beautiful analogy while climbing a sand dune in Saugatuck, Michigan.
» Had moments of truth clearly spoken to me.
» Began finding my voice even more than before.
» Had a vision of the number 38. (I was 35 when this vision came. At the time, I didn't know what this specific vision meant, but I now know that 38 ended up being the age that I published this book!)

Let me tell you that, although energy clearings, astrology, psychic readings, or anything else of that sort may be interesting (sometimes even tantalizing), my faith and belief in God far outweigh any of these. I do notice that bits and pieces of different readings I have had tend to stand out a little more than others, and I always wonder.

I had a psychic reading done around 2013, and I remember the woman telling me that I would get married and have kids of my own one day—but that I would travel first. I have always wanted to travel, to see and experience what the world has to offer, the beauty God has created both inside and outside of the United States. So, I started to wonder, *Is this my time to do so?*

The energy clearing, done in 2020, seemed to confirm that, once again, I would without a doubt marry and that my husband would love me unconditionally. Her description of him had been simple—tall and broad-shouldered—and she saw a school and church and told me that, when he hugs me, I will feel the safest I have ever felt and will feel secure in his love.

She also told me that she saw three children—two boys and one girl. I laughed because I thought, *Well, I'd better get started with the age I'm at!* But again, you never know! The plans God has for us are always so far beyond what we could imagine. My hope is in Him, not myself—and certainly not in an energy reading or in the way the stars align. My hope is in God, and I knew He was about to lead me on a journey nothing could have prepared me for!

PAUSE AND REFLECT

Ending a relationship can bring up a lot of emotion. When you think about a relationship that ended in your past,

- What emotions surfaced during that time?
- What support did you have as you were going through this loss and grieving the relationship?
- What steps did you take to move forward?
- What did you learn about yourself while going through this?

Part 3

DISCOVERING MY IDENTITY

chapter 11

The Journey Back to Him

I HAVE ALWAYS LOVED being outside. However, there was a span of time when I seemed to forget how essential this was. When the pandemic began, nature was my place of retreat and solitude. I found myself remembering how much I loved being surrounded by new life, watching things grow, and being immersed in fresh air. Nature is the place where I have always felt closest to God.

One September afternoon I drove to Saugatuck, a town along Lake Michigan, put on my day pack, and started walking. I didn't have a clue where I was going, but it didn't matter. I took in the sights, smells, and sounds of fresh water, people talking and laughing, and butterflies crossing my path. I saw a massive sand dune and knew I had to climb it.

As I did, I kept thinking to myself, *Climbing is a symbol of life.* We each have in mind a highest point, a "top" we feel we must reach, but the climb is usually challenging. At times you may have to walk on an angle, stepping onto a different path because climbing straight up is much more difficult. That straight path makes it hard to breathe at times, and the sand keeps sliding you down. It's almost as if you take one step forward and slide at least two steps back. You ask yourself, *What do I do now?*

You try to get off the straight path and veer to the side path, feeling that it's "safer." You feel as though you're making more progress on your climb to the summit, but then you recognize that you're traveling to the side and no longer going up, getting further away from your destination. It's time you make a choice: Keep going, knowing the side path will continue to take you further away, or go back, refocus, and go back to climbing straight up.

What the climb here on earth brings you is wisdom and reinforces your freedom to choose the path with God!

Sometimes you don't have to go all the way back. Sometimes all it takes is recognizing that you're off the path and believing you have the strength to resume climbing straight up. However, you don't realize right away that there might be unhealed wounds, losses, and grief from the other path. It's a continuous cycle, but the One who will always be by your side, whatever path you take, is God! You realize that God will always be there, pulling you back and forgiving you for trying to take an "easier" trail. This is the moment you forgive yourself for trying to take control of your life, acknowledging that you truly have no control! He gives you the free will to choose the route to take. I don't know about you, but I thank Him for that!

Even when you reach the highpoint, sometimes that destination is not what you had expected because it's not truly the top! It's not truly home because you aren't eternally Home yet. What the climb here on earth brings you is wisdom and reinforces your freedom to choose the path with God!

There will always be trials, challenges, and slipups, and sometimes it feels as though the sand is bringing you further and further down. What do you do? You grab onto whatever you can and remind yourself that you are a child of God. Then, when you reach the summit, you'll be able to sit, reflect, and be present in the moment. You know that, if you go back down, this downward trail will be "easy" and freeing . . . for a time. But you don't want to miss what God has planned for you.

It was on that sand dune that it clicked for me: I had chosen the Lord's path. I didn't want to go back down a path I'd already been on, a path with obstacles I'd already overcome and didn't want to relive, though I did want to grow from those experiences. I wanted to be a better version of who God had created me to be.

As I sat on the top of the dune overlooking miles of water, boats, and people, all looking like toys, I let go of my past and felt the strength to continue to climb upward, toward my Lord and Savior. I prayed,

> *Thank You, Lord, for this time. For my life, for this space, for these moments to find myself again. To find my identity in You, accepting my reality exactly as it is, without any visions of what I should have or what I want in life right now. I have an abundant life brimming and overflowing with love, relationships, peace, serving, amazing health, a cozy home, and the ability to be free in every aspect. It's time to transform and fly again!*

There are underlying themes I took away from this time that are important for me, and for you, to keep in mind:

» Life is not easy, but growth makes living more beautiful.
» You always have the choice, the free will, to decide which path to take.
» Accept reality wherever you are.
» The expectations you put on yourself, especially regarding relationships, need to be replaced with God's peace. You are right where you need to be for a reason, and you need to accept that reality and grow from there.
» Suffering is normal and expected. And within that suffering wisdom will surface. Rewards, beauty, and breathtaking moments will result!
» Life is a journey worth taking.

Repeat after me . . .

This is normal.

I'm not alone.

God will meet me here.

I spent the next few months listening to podcasts, reading, praying, refocusing, reflecting, and preparing for the next chapter in my life: singleness and the gift it is!

The Gift of Singleness

A gift is given for different reasons and for many occasions. The gift is usually something the giver thought would make you smile, make your day, or make you feel special. Why, then, does society portray singleness as anything but a gift? I have learned along my journey that singleness is truly a gift, and it's a choice to see it as such.

As I begin this part of my story, I will say now that there were men I talked to during the year, and I tried online dating sites again, after vowing not to. There was one guy I felt a connection to, but the timing wasn't right. Just as with any gift, you don't know what you have received until you open it. Once you do, and after the excitement dies down, you step back and reflect on the reason behind the gift. There's always a reason.

I cannot tell you the reason behind my many years of singleness. But I also haven't felt sorry for myself (okay, maybe sometimes) for not having what so many others do: a partner and/or a child or children of my own. Though it hasn't always been easy, I have learned to remind myself to trust the process, to lean into where I am and where God is leading me. If it weren't for this time of singleness, I would not be the woman I am today.

From the moment we are born, most of us are surrounded by love. We are brought into this world helpless, innocent, pure, and unable to live without love. As we develop and grow, love is there in different forms, in different ways, at different times. It may not be as obvious as in that moment fresh from the womb, but it is there. We strive to be accepted and loved. This striving continues as we grow from infancy into childhood and from adolescence into adulthood. It doesn't go away, and that is okay.

Our society and culture make love out to be a fairytale.

Cute boy meets cute girl.

Boy pursues girl.

Girl falls "head over heels" in love with boy.
Boy and girl fight.
Boy realizes his stupidity.
Boy apologizes to girl.
Girl forgives boy and takes him back.
Boy proposes to girl.
Girl plans a $50,000 wedding.
Boy and girl marry.
Boy and girl buy a house.
Boy and girl have a baby.
Boy and girl live happily ever after.

Did you notice that I never changed the nouns? Boy and Girl. This is the culturally and societally accepted formula for looking at love. This is the process, the chronological "next steps" society tells us boys and girls should follow. We see it in the books we read and in movies we watch, but I am here to tell you it's a false construct.

I know, of course, that this type of love story happens. This boy and girl grow and mature together, and eventually the boy and girl become man and woman together. If this is you, I offer you congratulations as you share life together through all its ups and downs. But would you agree that the going hasn't always been easy? In my opinion different perspectives on life and love need to be shared and celebrated!

Love is hard work. Love can be hurtful. Love brings together two different people with two different mindsets, two different perspectives, and two different sets of life experience. It has taken me years of undoing this fairytale thinking to realize this, and yet I still believe in love!

I continue to have moments of asking "When?"

» When will it be my turn?
» When will I feel love with and for a man who makes me feel safe and cherished?
» When will I get to experience the ultrasound picture, the first heartbeat, the precious little miracle that God has created and whom I now cradle in my arms?

The answer: I don't know.

No one does.

No one is guaranteed any of this. That's the hard truth. Life is a journey to find peace, to appreciate our individual path, to focus on small achievements and happy moments that allow us to recover strength after that yearning ache of "When?" so we can keep moving forward. We are given our special, one-of-a-kind life . . . to *live*! Through the mess, the hurt, the questions, the anger, and the loss, it's our choice whether we want to embrace our singleness or wallow in it, feeling sorry for ourselves. I chose to embrace it and see where God would lead me.

In November 2020, I listened to a podcast in which the host interviewed a woman who put some things into perspective for me. The title of the podcast was *Time and Energy Management for Ambitious Women (Better! With Dr. Stephanie)*. My takeaways:

- We are not what we produce.
- Life is truly a cycle. We're not going anywhere, but just cycling through.
- I'm a recovering overachiever and perfectionist.
- Be the egg.

Let me explain the egg, based on this episode. Did you know that we women are born with all the egg cells we will ever have? We go through a 28 day-ish monthly cycle broken into four seasons, each with certain tendencies. Each one of our eggs has a strong boundary, stays exactly where it's supposed to be, and allows sperm to penetrate only when it's time. How does this apply in terms of an analogy to our own lives? How often do we find ourselves wanting to do more, to be more, to control more instead of just staying put until it's time?

Be the egg. Be still and confident in the waiting. God provides for us and sends things our way only when He knows we're ready. I believe this because I've witnessed it many times in my life. We need to remind ourselves to embrace the waiting and to trust the process. We know we will attract the people and outcomes God has planned for us, but only when it's time and when we're emotionally, mentally, and spiritually ready.

What if we were to learn and apply this perspective on our egg cells to our lives? What might it look like for us to set strong boundaries and open ourselves up only when we feel it's time? Without this gift of singleness, I know that I would not have encountered this perspective on my eggs! Let me tell you, those eggs are tough . . . and so am I!

The year 2021 brought travel, self-love, and an abundance of *courage*, which happened to be my word for that year. I also started the year off reaching out to someone on Instagram. Here's the quick backstory.

I was talking to my friend Joe as I drove to my parents' house for the holidays. (Quick reminder: Joe has been in my life for years. He's the one I refer to as my "Hitch.") During our conversation, I remember him telling me that, if his brother could find a woman like me, he would be incredibly lucky! I had gone to college with one of his brothers, but I hadn't met the youngest brother. I thought, *It doesn't hurt to check him out on Instagram*, which I did.

At the beginning of January, I sent him a message, and we started chatting a bit. Miles was up front and honest with me that he was going through a tough breakup and wasn't in the best place to think about women. I told him that I understood and respected him for telling me. He messaged me later, saying that, when he is in a better state, he would love to continue to get to know me because I seemed like a great woman.

I prayed that God would give me patience and show Miles the respect he deserved in figuring out stuff with his ex. The one thing I knew was that I did not want to get into another relationship in which the other person was not ready or able to be all in. I know we all heal at different rates, and I have learned that there's no set length for healing; it could be four months or three years in any particular situation. It's important to take the necessary time to refocus on ourselves, learn and reflect on the relationship, and trust that God, in His time, will reveal if and when both people are ready.

So, I prayed. I prayed about my singleness. I knew in my heart that I was single for many reasons. I prayed that God would someday satisfy the desire of my heart to have a fulfilling, loving marriage that only He could orchestrate. I prayed not only for patience in the waiting but also for my future husband. I prayed that, if marriage were indeed part of His plan, God would prepare both of our hearts, minds, bodies, and souls as we continued to learn more about Him, ourselves, our significant other, and our relationship, all of which are important to our living out God's plan, both now in our singleness and, if within His will for us, in our marriage someday.

And was God preparing me in every way!

There was back-and-forth communication between Miles and me for the next month or so. We Zoomed a few times for a couple of hours and talked on the phone; I had never been particularly comfortable with phone conversations but never knew why, until it hit me one day after hanging up with Miles. I had spent hours upon hours on the phone with Scammer. All of it had been a lie. I had shared so much with this person, and phone conversations were all that we'd had—because that was all he'd given me.

Fast forward to the present, and I found myself actually enjoying and looking forward to my conversations with Miles. I felt that our conversations were healthy interactions and that he genuinely cared. In one conversation we shared our faith and beliefs. I remember getting off the call and feeling my gut kick in about the way I had expressed myself regarding my faith. I knew this would have to be a continued conversation because, although I felt affirmed, I also noticed that my gut (Hello, Holy Spirit!) was making itself known again and I committed, at the beginning of 2021, to listening to it the first time.

Miles was not exactly sure where he stood in his faith, and I found myself wrestling a bit with this. I knew in my heart that the relationship I wanted would have to have a foundation in Christ. It took me years to fully admit this to myself, but I truly believe that God is preparing me for a relationship beyond what I can imagine. "Faith," I remind myself, "is confidence in what we hope for and assurance about what we do not see" Hebrews 11:1 (NIV).

I started praying for Miles in February 2021 that he would find his way back to God and experience a relationship with Jesus Christ. In the meantime, I realized that I had to start working through the shameful things I did as a child and tackling the healing from the sexual trauma I had gone through as a young adult.

Sexual trauma looks different for every individual. My story is not yours and vice versa. However, after years of therapy, life coaching, and reading *The Body Keeps the Score* by Bessel van der Kolk, I realize and acknowledge that what I endured was sexual trauma, along with emotional and mental abuse. I had held on to so much guilt and shame for so long. Do you know the difference between these emotions?

» Guilt is feeling that a behavior you did was wrong or bad.
» Shame is when you feel that *you* are bad because of the things you said or did.

Imagine experiencing this shame and guilt as a 10-year-old and carrying it until you are 23 years old. There are so many shameful memories, so many moments of feeling that I was being punished for what I had done as a little girl and that I deserved punishment. The memories, thoughts, and negative self-talk had woven their way deep into my neurons. Because of this, I felt as though I would never be worthy of a relationship. I felt dirty and unclean. As a little girl I tried to release all of this shame to our priest. I had been raised Catholic, and everything I had been taught about sex I had heard and interpreted as bad: *Don't have sex until you're married. You are dirty if you do anything sexual, etc.*

I overthought all of this and felt as though I were going to hell. Once I confessed to the priest, I was given Hail Mary's to recite in the hope that my sin would wash away. I figured that this would wash away my thoughts and memories of the sin, too. I didn't want my sin to be a part of me any longer, but I felt as though it had never gone away.

I felt that I was bad. I had even gone through a resentful phase, feeling as though I were doing all the prescribed "things" but that none of them seemed to help. The thoughts and feelings kept cycling over and over again through my mind. I felt as though God were punishing me, while in fact I was the one punishing myself and never letting it go.

A pattern surfaced later on, linking drinking or getting drunk with being intimate with a guy. Because it was never talked about, I had never recognized my sexuality as something positive, as a gift to be cherished. Every time I drank, I was running from the hurt. I would wake up the next day feeling even dirtier . . . and hung over on top of it. This behavior reinforced my spiral of not viewing sexuality as something beautiful, romantic, and sacred.

How many of you have heard statements like the following?

Everyone is doing it.
It's part of human desire.
It's your passage into adulthood.
Why are you waiting?
You're a prude.
You've already had sex, so why hold out in your new relationship?
You're too innocent.
One night stand.
Lust and passion equal love.
If you have sex before marriage, you will feel so much shame and dirtiness.
By the end of the night, I'll be banging her.
Do you think this outfit will get me laid?
Let's go back to my place and I'll show you a good time!
Oh, you're such a goody-two-shoes.

I've heard it all. And I've felt it all. When you just want to fit in, be liked, and to feel good enough, you will do pretty much anything to hide from your intuition that keeps telling you, *No, don't do it.* Full disclosure: I fell for it. I fell, and it never felt right.

I shared earlier that I had lost my virginity at the age of 27. I had been drinking and drove to the home of a guy I'd had an interest in. We drank more, made out, . . . and one thing led to another. I remember driving home from that one-night stand feeling anything but full or beautiful. I felt used, especially because the guy didn't really talk to me afterward.

Yet again, I felt full of shame and angry at myself. I was still talking to Scammer when this happened, and when I told him about it, he made me feel even more ashamed. He couldn't believe I would "give in" like that. I remember standing at my apartment door, fumbling with my keys as my inner little girl felt beat up, unworthy of a guy, and unworthy to be loved. I felt broken and hurt. But I still believed in love!

I remember both of the men I've had sex with because they have each taken a small part of me in a way others haven't. Sex is not meant to make you feel dirty, shameful, or guilty. The act is meant to be beautiful and something intimate between two people, an expression of the love that connects them. I feel that our culture has made this vision into a fantasy rather than reality, which makes me feel unworthy.

However, I have hope because I believe that sexual intimacy should be a huge part of marriage once you feel fully connected spiritually, emotionally, and mentally. We need to start embracing this and talking to our young daughters and sons, our teens, and young women and men so they can feel comfortable in their own skin. So they will not feel dirty or experience the shame many of us have felt from our past and might still feel today. I knew that God had given me this time to heal and to prepare me to experience such a beautiful connection someday, no matter how hard it was to wait.

I was digging deeply into the issue at the time and realized more acutely that Scammer and the relationship he had made appear so real were in fact leading me deeper and deeper into a hole. All along I could see a sliver of light—which I never lost sight of—but the darkness, the exposing videos, the hurt, the lost time, and the vulnerability I had been allowing as I was being crushed, manipulated, and gaslighted overwhelmed my psyche, and I continued to feel that I wasn't enough.

This was all so hard to process. The videos exposed me and, once again, made me feel dirty and emotionally abused. The images felt almost seared into my mind. Scammer always wanted and asked for more, not listening to how uncomfortable these demands were making me feel. It—or I—was never enough. I wanted (and honestly know that I still want) someone to pull me close and reassure me that these feelings are okay. Acknowledging hurt helps us get through it and is far better than hurting ourselves more and more with narratives engraved on our minds from long ago. Our words, thoughts, and feelings will flow continuously, but the love we show ourselves is the true work that will allow us, fully and finally, to be set free!

Butterflies have been special to me since my grandma passed away. On the day of her funeral, I remember praying that God would give me a sign that she was still in our presence. Shortly after that prayer, a butterfly flew by. It wasn't until 2016 and that period of growth that I deepened my connection to butterflies in a whole new way. I remember a session with Michelle when she told me that I had been encased in my cocoon for so long but had finally broken free. It was time to fly! I had the world to explore, and my transformation was just beginning. I didn't know where life would lead me. I still don't, but that's all part of the journey.

Butterflies must be patient and resilient as they transform. Many friends told me after I had been scammed how resilient I was. I felt the truth of that but didn't truly understand. It wasn't until Michelle explained to me about post-traumatic growth (PTG) that I started to recognize how resilient I truly am. I began reading more about PTG and discovered that it's not only about overcoming trauma but also about growing past it.

The concept of post-traumatic growth defined what I had been feeling. But such growth takes work and doesn't happen overnight. Growth is a lifelong process, but it's worth the investment of time, energy, and strength because you are reminded of it daily in terms of a recognition of where you were, where you had thought you would be, and where you are now—which is the beauty of it all.

It was time for my unpacking to begin. Unpacking from a trip or a move takes time. It takes time to take everything out of boxes, making sure to be gentle with fragile things, and to find a place for each item. It also takes time to put something back where it came from. It's okay to rearrange things and toss out items you no longer need or that don't bring you joy any longer. You may even purchase new items to make your space feel more like home. It's a process to fully unpack from a trip or make a place your home. Honestly, it's a job that's never done. But it's healthy! I knew in 2016 that I was not ready to unpack all of what I have shared because I was just trying to survive. The time eventually came, though, to do so.

> "Don't keep going over old history . . . I'm about to do something brand-new." Isaiah 43:18–19 (MSG)

God opened my heart again to love, but I also prayed that I would discipline myself to listen to His voice, that I would let Him lead me. I knew that the men He had so far put into my life had been journey partners who had helped shape me. It was time to lean into these experiences, to forgive myself for sins that we had committed while together, and to begin to date and love one person before anyone else . . . myself!

On Valentine's Day 2021, I committed to dating and loving myself by enjoying places, nature, and time with God. I began to embrace the gift of singleness and the woman God had created me to be—strong, resilient, kind, compassionate, forgiving, funny, sarcastic, genuine, authentic, and courageous. This commitment began my journey of finding contentment in the love only God can provide. Although at times I still prayed for my future husband, my prayers became more about beginning the journey of finding contentment in God's love.

> *Lord, take my worry, anxiousness, wondering, curiosity, love, hope, and faith, as I wait patiently for what You bring to me today. I want to be content in every way. I pray about my longing to be in a relationship and have a family of my own. I am reminded of my relationship with You and of all that You have given me. I truly am blessed and satisfied. I still pray for the desire to appreciate and live out my life fully, in the present moment, every day.*

I found myself communicating with God in prayer more frequently, sharing with Him my struggles, hurts, anger, thoughts, joys, wants, and desires. This is when I found myself truly letting go and letting God take the wheel.

- How might you describe yourself at this time in your life? Now think about how God would describe you, the person He created you to be.
- Are those descriptions similar or different?
- What might be holding you back from seeing yourself as God sees you?
- What steps might you consider to help you release the past and fly freely into the future?

chapter 12

You Have to Start Somewhere

MY MOM TELLS me my birth story every year.

The Quick Version:

My mom went into labor with me.

My dad was working on the west side of the state and had to drive three hours in a blizzard to get to the hospital.

My mom told the nurse that she had to wait for my dad to get there, but the nurse looked down and responded, "Um, there's no waiting! I see a head!"

I was ready to enter this world, and no one was going to stop me!

I love this story for many reasons. I now realize how my birth symbolizes my life.

- When I put my mind to something, I make it happen.
- I am determined to get things done.
- I can be stubborn at times and often think about others before myself.

- I don't stay in one place for too long because life is full of adventures. You have to be willing to make a move, even though you might not know the outcome.
- My parents will always be there to support, encourage, and love me, no matter how far apart we might be.

From the moment I was born, I have waited for no one!

In March 2021 I made one of my Vision Board dreams a reality: I took a long weekend and visited Savannah, Georgia. The beauty, history, warmth, and freedom I felt while walking, exploring, and meeting new people will always hold a special place in my heart.

My word for 2021: Courage.

It took courage to tell my parents I was taking this trip and doing it by myself.

It took courage to set foot in an airport when the world had been shut down for over a year due to the COVID-19 pandemic.

It took courage to invite a young traveler who had lost his mother to cancer several months earlier to join me at a restaurant when I was planning to eat by myself. If I hadn't invited this stranger over, I would not have heard his story, started following his journey across the U.S. on Instagram, and encouraged him to live and dream big.

Throughout the four-day trip, I sat at a rooftop bar for hours, did a lot of journaling, and treated myself to a delicious charcuterie board and drinks while listening to live music as the sun warmed my face and I met two women having a Sunday Funday next to me. I found myself walking through the park, stopping at the fountain, standing in line for ice cream, exploring this historic town on a trolley ride, and stopping at SCAD (Savannah College of Art and Design) to admire the beautiful student art on display.

I arrived in Savannah giggling at myself as I walked from downtown to the Airbnb—through not the safest part of town—with my rolling carry-on trailing behind me. (Don't worry, Mom and Dad—it was still light out!) I left Savannah after first feeding and then praying for a homeless woman at a coffee shop I had stopped at while waiting for my Uber to take me to the airport.

I had arrived in Savannah with courage in my heart. And I left Savannah with my heart full and ready for whatever more this world had to offer!

Since reading the bestseller *Eat, Pray, Love* by Elizabeth Gilbert, I had wanted to experience an adventure like Elizabeth did. It hit me as I flew home that this Savannah adventure was the beginning of my own *Eat, Pray, Love* experience. My adventures would take me to other places and teach me more about my faith, about healing, and about self-love.

I put the details of my next adventure into God's hands, praying daily for affordable flights and a safe Airbnb. He led me to book a trip to Scottsdale, Arizona, for spring break!

The day I flew to Scottsdale, I felt frustrated about relationships. Though I was finding contentment in life and in my healing journey, the desire for connection and love from a significant other was still surfacing. Instead of sitting in these feelings, I prayed. I prayed to be engulfed with God's everyday beauty and surrounded by His unconditional love. I prayed for the people I would meet in Scottsdale. Although my mind seemed to be on constant alert for a man, I prayed that He would help me turn off that jarring voice and be present in my experiences and with myself. Singleness can be a beautiful journey and, although I was feeling frustrated, I wanted to embrace this gift!

I also continued to pray for my future husband. You might be feeling or doing something similar. If so, I encourage you to pray this prayer . . .

> *I pray, God, that You are preparing my future husband and myself for love, a partnership, and a relationship only You can orchestrate. Continue to prepare our hearts, minds, bodies, and souls, spiritually, emotionally, mentally, and physically. Help us to come together as one, with You as our solid foundation. I pray that my future husband will be a man who leads by faith, loves by grace, forgives without judging or holding grudges, and loves You more than anyone else, including me.*
>
> *I pray that my future husband shows strength in his weaknesses, continues to heal his inner wounds, shows his*

love in the small ways, and wants to always continue to grow individually and together with You in his/our faith. I pray, Lord, that You will choose my future husband and bring us together at the right time. In the waiting, help me to remain patient and focused on loving others, on being Your light, serving wherever You lead me and embracing the moments You have planned for my days, weeks, months, and the years ahead.

My four days in Scottsdale brought warm sunshine, dry heat, lots of walking, trying new coffee shops and restaurants, and meeting many people along the way. I relished the beauty surrounding me every day. The place where I stayed had a beautiful little patio where I spent my mornings eating breakfast, drinking cups of coffee, and engaging in my quiet time. I spent Easter Sunday in this space, watching a church service online with the sun rising, purple flowers and vines climbing up the white walls as a backdrop, and feeling God's comforting Spirit reminding me of the sacrifice Christ made for me to be here in this moment.

I was and am free of the shame and guilt of my past sins, of the sins I commit each day, and of the sins I will commit in the future. My journey in seeking out a relationship with Jesus Christ had begun fourteen years earlier when I moved to South Carolina. Although I was physically in Scottdale by myself, I knew I wasn't alone.

With every step I took on this trip, I remember feeling peace that I couldn't describe. With every step I took I embraced the sounds, smells, tastes, and people I observed and engaged with in conversation. Every step I took was a gift that healed my inner soul from all the hurt, turmoil, anxiety, negative thoughts, shame, guilt, and the inner critic that had held me back all my life! Every step I took was freeing and necessary to get me where I am today.

Give yourself time to answer this question:

Where are your steps taking you?

On my second morning I woke up early, hopped into an Uber, and made the twenty-minute drive to Camelback Mountain, well known for its hiking trails. I was advised to get there at around 6:00 a.m., to bring lots of water, and to enjoy the views. I was also told that there were usually a couple of emergency rescues each day due to heat exhaustion and not having enough water. Little did I know what I was about to experience. Imagine large boulders, rough surfaces, no easy way up, and challenges every step of the way. The Lord knew I was up for the challenge! I could conquer this rocky mountain just as I had every other rocky part in my life.

I was not in a rush.

I walked.

I jumped on and off boulders, crawling my way up at certain points.

I encouraged others as I passed them or when I was struggling to catch my breath on the way to the next stopping point.

I stopped to snap photos, some far off the well-traveled path.

I was surrounded by mountains, cacti, bees, desert, and hot air, and by the time I got to the top the morning sun was shining brightly, almost like God's victory light celebrating that I had made it! As I stood on a large boulder while setting the self-timer to capture photos depicting the strength I was feeling, I looked out and saw a world that only God could have created! I was in awe at how high up I was, looking at the world below me, where everything looked miniature. This was the true definition of a bird's-eye view.

At one point in my climb, I remember looking up and seeing people the size of ants moving up the mountain in front of me. I felt the same way when I looked down the mountain at the houses and miles of the unknown. As I sat there taking in the view in both directions, I thought about how small we truly are in this world.

Why is there so much hatred and dislike, when there's so much beauty and natural peace surrounding us? I remember thinking, *I don't want to be oblivious or naïve to what goes on in this world, but I don't want to surround myself with it, either.* It might be easier on vacation to find these peaceful moments, but I prayed that I wouldn't forget them when daily life resumed. I prayed that I would live my life fully in the present, feeling God's love and goodness embracing me every step of the way, just as I was doing in that moment and had done in the steps I had taken to get there.

After I had snapped some photos and taken in the 360° view, I found a spot on a rock and pulled out my journal. That was when I noticed a chipmunk. This little creature with his nose moving so quickly sat within a foot or so of me, waiting for me to either feed it or move out of its space. In this moment I felt beyond grateful, so at peace and in awe of this time to experience new places, people, and nature.

The experience was a reminder that the Lord had plans for me, at least at this moment, that didn't necessarily involve being married and having children of my own. I took time to reflect on where I had been a year earlier. I had been celebrating Easter with Jay and continuing my journey toward knowing God more intimately. I was impressed in this moment by the personal relationship I had discovered with God. He is the One and Only who will never let us down.

He is the One and Only who will never let us down.

My prayer for all of us is that we will continue experiencing this amazing, precious life God gives us daily and never take it for granted. He provides each one of us so much beauty and love. The question is, *Are we taking time to listen and take it all in?*

As I began my trek down the mountain, I felt the heat rising and understood the advice I had been given. I was thankful I had begun my hike early. At one point a mother stopped and asked me, "Are we almost to the top?" I smiled and encouraged, "You have a long way to go, but all it takes is one step at a time!"

I was almost down the mountain when I remembered thinking that some of these people just starting their hike were in for a challenge. I prayed that they had enough water to make it to the top and back in the heat that seemed in itself to climb every minute. When I approached a flatter area, I came upon another mother with her three children. A couple of them had climbed up on the boulders, and one seemed to be stuck, contemplating how to get down. The mother looked up at him and asked a simple question, "How can I help you?"

Those five words made me rethink the way I have questioned children—and anyone who has seemed to be struggling or in need of help in some way. How many times do we as adults jump in to fix a situation for our children, grandchildren, students, significant others, friends, family, etc.? I realized that asking this question allows the other person to *think* about what they truly need. It makes them consider possible solutions to the problem they face.

This interaction also made me think about wait time. We don't like to wait. We'd much rather resolve a dilemma right away or immediately fix a problem for someone else; after all, we have things to do as we run from one task to the next. However, asking this question requires a pause . . . some time to be uncomfortable in the silence. This pause gives the other person time to assess what they really need. Often in the pause they discover that they have ownership of their own problem. They may then ask you for specific support or encouragement rather than expecting you to solve their problem for them right away. We need to stop rescuing and instead start embracing the pause and encouraging more think time.

I was deep in thought the rest of the way down the mountain, in awe of this mother's strength. She knew her child was safe, but what she would never know was how that question had impacted me, a fellow hiker passing by for thirty seconds. This moment demonstrated for me how inner strength can persevere; I was impacted by how this mother helped her child think for himself, which helped create in him independence.

Thirty seconds.

A simple question.

A reframing that provided a challenge.

This event also reminded me of the book *Think Again* by Adam Grant. Grant made me rethink a lot, especially related to courageous and crucial conversations, those conversations you don't want to have but know will grow you—and possibly the other person—in the process. The conversations in which not everyone may end up agreeing, but all will understand that this is okay as long as a culture of safety, vulnerability, and respect is established and maintained.

These conversations are not easy, but they are often necessary. *Crucial Conversations: Tools for Talking When Stakes are High*, by Joseph Grenny, Kerry Patterson, Ron McMillan, Al Switzler, and Emily

Gregory, is another great resource that gives you tools to recognize when conversations turn crucial and what you can do instead of freezing or fleeing.

The day after the hike I treated myself to a spa day at The Scott Resort & Spa. I lounged by the pool, soaked in a copper tub before getting a much-needed massage, and finished my time at the resort in the Canal Club. I listened to light music playing in the background and the sounds of the bartender making drinks as I began journaling.

I wrote about the 83-year-old man I had met on Camelback Mountain as I was hiking up and he was coming down. He had told me that his secret for staying young was taking Vitamin C for his joints and to ward off varicose veins. I wrote about the couple I met at the pool who were teachers from Michigan. We shared the hardships we faced in education and the joy we felt being in Arizona taking a break from it all.

I also wrote about Ed and Val, a couple staying at my Airbnb. We had a beautiful conversation on the patio one morning about our faith and relationships. I also met an older gentleman at the bar on my way back to the Airbnb from the spa day. He was a regular, and all the staff at the restaurant knew him. I listened to his stories and could tell he might have had a form of dementia, but it was apparent that he was loved and cared for at that bar by the whole staff.

God blesses you with people when you least expect it. Although our paths crossed only briefly, each one of these individuals is part of my story. Each one of them added to the beauty of my life via the conversations we had. You never know what a simple smile or hello will bring, but I was finding out that it's worth it every time to make the small effort.

On my last night in Scottsdale, I walked to a brewery I had heard about. I observed new establishments being built, along with the noise and busyness of an up-and-coming area. When I arrived, I chose a spot at the outdoor bar. I was enjoying the views, listening to the music, and watching people.

Soon a man came in and sat on the other side of the bar. He was attractive, solo, and didn't have a ring on (think what you may, but that tends to be one of my first looks). I was finishing my beer when I noticed he was cashing out. I would be lying if I said I didn't keep my eye on him throughout the night. Instead of walking out the door, he walked toward me!

"Hi! I'm Steven. You seem to have a good energy, and I wanted to come and say hi."

"Well, I'm glad you did!" I responded.

Our conversation lasted about five minutes. Steven was in town for a conference and said he enjoyed trying new places. I told him that I was a teacher on spring break, and we eventually got to talking about the book I had recently started to write. He told me he had written a book himself and would be happy to send me a copy.

Without this five-minute interaction, I wouldn't have received a signed copy of *The 7 Rocks of Life: The Key to Filling Up Your Life Cup* by Steven Mazzurco, which he wrote so authentically to connect with his readers. As I got into the Uber that evening, the driver was playing Christian music, and one of my favorite songs came on. I felt God telling me that He was right there with me and would be with me even through the challenging, stubborn moments I would face when I sat down and continued to write my story.

There have been so many roadblocks and voices in my head telling me that what I write doesn't sound right or make any sense, or that it won't make a difference. I have felt afraid of bringing up the hurt and pain, but I also know the calling I feel to help others feel less alone in their quests for and along their journeys of love. I prayed that I would lean into the human fear and replace it with the fear only God provides. Yes, there is a difference!

Merriam-Webster.com defines *fear* as "an unpleasant, often strong emotion caused by anticipation or awareness of danger." This is human fear, which tends to cause anxiety, concern, and alarm. However, *fear of God* is defined as a "profound reverence and awe" for what He provides. As the character Mulan, in the Disney movie by the same name, said, "There is no courage without fear."

It was time to dive deeply and continue writing my story. Another solo adventure was in the books, and it was time to begin my next one.

PAUSE AND REFLECT

Think about some of the places you've been, times in your life when you've had to start over, and the people you've met along the way.

- In what ways have you grown after these encounters?
- What are some things you discovered about yourself and others during these times?

chapter 13

Post-Traumatic Growth (PTG) Is Continuous Work . . . Keep Going

I'M A QUOTE person. I love quotes. I connect to quotes. And sometimes I find myself watching a show or reading a book only to pause and write down what the actor/actress or author said.

Grey's Anatomy has always been a favorite show. Yes, I am one of the rare ones who has watched all nineteen—yes, nineteen seasons. The relationships, the connections, and every character's journey have been fun to watch unfold. There was one episode (Season 17, Episode 10) where Lexi, Mark Sloan, and Meredith were talking about change and relationships:

Mark: "What's the thing that caused the pain?"

Lexi: "The depth of grief that you felt with the losses; it's because of the depth of love. As long as you're alive, you get to feel it and you get to do something about it. Everything changes all the time when you're alive, and all the time you fight the change. You cling onto what you have and what you know like that's how it should always be."

Mark: "It's such a waste of life."
Lexi: "Right?"
Meredith: "What's a waste?"
Mark: "Fighting change."
Lexi: "Resisting pain. Don't waste it, Meredith."
Meredith: "Waste what?"
Mark: "Don't waste a single minute."

Pain and grief can come when you least expect them. Now, in this in-between interim, I continued to lean into both because I knew from experience that on the other side was freedom. I love and trust deeply, knowing that there's always the chance I could get hurt in the process. However, without love we have nothing. I prayed for an increase in my love for God, my love for others, and my love for myself.

Without love, we have nothing.

We all want to be loved, to feel loved, and to give love. Throughout this time I realized even more what love truly is. According to Paul in 1 Corinthians 13,

- Love is pure and genuine. It never gives up.
- Love is a choice. You have to *put love on* every day.
- Love is an action. You cannot just talk about it; you have to do it! You have to act on it. As the saying goes, "Actions speak louder than words."

One thing we do to show love is to absolve offenses. Love is beautiful, but it can also break and destroy. I'd rather love hard than waste my life fighting, resisting, and shielding the hurt and pain I feel along the way. I believe in the power of love and the feeling of love, and I pray that someday I will experience more deeply the love from God that protects me, supports me, encourages me, and does life with me. It's a love that never dies.

As humans, we strive for clarity and thrive when issues are clear in our minds.

How many times have you desired clarity regarding a situation, a relationship that has ended, or a decision that was made? As humans, we strive for clarity and thrive when issues are clear in our minds. Clarity came for me one night in May. A clarity I didn't know I needed but one that I am so glad I received.

I was with some friends celebrating the cancer remission of one amazingly strong woman, mother, and wife. There were drinks, laughter, lots of catching up, and massive amounts of tears flowing from me. The four of us were sitting around the outside fire when Stella looked at me and apologized for everything that had happened between me and Greg. I asked her if she knew that Greg had sent me a letter and had tried contacting me a few times after we had broken up. She said that there was so much she wanted to tell me, but only if I wanted to hear it. Knowing where I was in my PTG journey, I definitely was ready.

That night I found out that Greg had been struggling and had been uncertain about whether to go to Dominican Republic with me even before we left! His sisters had warned him not to go and then break my heart afterward! His sisters, extended family, and even his dad (whom I met only once) had told him that he would regret breaking up with me and advised him not to do it.

Needless to say, I had been the one who'd had the courage to bring up the possibility and talk about it after we got back. Even after returning, he hadn't seemed to be moving fast to end things. Stella then told me that Greg had since bought a house down the street from them with a woman who had college-age kids. Not long afterward they had put it up for sale, and Stella thought he was living with one of his sisters for the time being.

As I sat there taking all this in, I was in shock. I sat there bawling, literally bawling out all the tears that had been held captive for the last three years! I remember thinking, *This is what I needed to hear. This is the closure I needed to finally move forward!* Stella and our other friends consoled me, yet the tears kept falling. My thoughts connected the timeline of events that had happened years earlier: Greg had written me that letter after ending things with one girl and had then texted me months after he had broken things off with this other girl he had bought a house with! *What?* Amidst the tears, hurt, and anger, I prayed for him. I prayed for his healing, for the Lord to direct him on the path He had for him. I also prayed that I could finally let him go, knowing that I am stronger because of what I went through with him, even after finding out all this.

I drove home that night in tears. I walked into my condo and found the journal and reread entries from when Greg and I had been dating, specifically around the time we took our trip to the Dominican Republic. Reading through those entries put them into a different perspective but also solidified my feelings from and about that trip. The disconnect I had felt from him. The anxiety I felt as soon as we were back at the airport and turned on our phones, me wondering right away if his ex-girlfriend had texted him. It all came together. I let the tears fall because I knew I needed to! I was angry, hurt, and sad. I knew that all of these emotions would settle in due time when I allowed myself to sit and process the situation more fully.

Sometimes one of the hardest parts of a breakup is gradually releasing connections with your ex's family members. I remember meeting up with one of Greg's sisters after we had broken things off. I remember feeling almost as though it had been a double break up, even though these others had done nothing wrong. However, I knew it wasn't the healthiest for us to continue to connect.

After our first meeting I realized this, and Greg's sister supported my setting a boundary for the time being so I could continue to heal and move forward. She understood. She said, "You deserve a prince! When you're ready, I would love to continue to hear about where you are in life, who you end up marrying, etc." And she genuinely meant it. After the most recent information, I knew I was in a place to connect with her again. I met up with her a couple of months later.

We caught up on our lives, and I found out that Greg had recently gotten engaged, which, to be honest, was more shocking to me than anything else. However, it shouldn't have been a surprise because, after me, it sounded as though he had gone from one girl to another. All while trying to contact me a few times, saying similar things each time but not fully admitting any of what I had more recently found out. Bottom line, he wasn't being honest. Trust had been broken years earlier, but it wasn't until this moment that I knew how much I had grown through it all.

The year 2021 was about healing, processing, growing, having, showing, and living my faith. It was about loving wholeheartedly, which included the one person I needed to love before I could ever love a significant other . . . myself.

Wisdom. Understanding. Knowledge. Fullness!

> "By wisdom a house is built, and through understanding it is established; through knowledge its rooms are filled with rare and beautiful treasures." Proverbs 24:3–4 (NIV)

God's wisdom is the basis of life. His wisdom is pretty clear, but what gets in the way are our desires and needs. Once you step back and begin to understand the life you've been given, your knowledge of living how God intends for you to live becomes clear. This clarity leads you to the beautiful treasures that make up your life.

As my wisdom in God's Word grew, so did my faith and trust in Him. The little moments led me to understand the power of trusting God. I had a tug on my heart around Mother's Day different from any I'd ever experienced before. I also attempted to go back on a couple of dating websites to see who was out there; I met some guys along the way, but none of them felt right. God's wisdom, my understanding of how it plays out in my everyday life, and my slowly beginning to realize the knowledge behind both things led me to the point of peace, love, forgiveness, and fullness!

Life has a "timeline" for us . . .

- As a child we wish to be older, and we wish our way out of innocence.
- As a teenager we wish to become independent by starting a job and/or beginning college.
- As a young adult we wish to become successful as we launch not just a job but a career. We experience dating; relationships; heartbreak; love; and, for some of us, marriage.
- The next "step" in this societal timeline is to have children.

What happens when this "timeline" doesn't unfold for us the way we'd like it to?

For me, there have been many questions and feelings of not being good enough; shame as "punishment" for my lack of relational happiness; and, at age 38, the question *Will I experience what society views as an "appropriate timeline" for living a full life?*

I know I am not the only one who has these feelings and thoughts racing through her mind. The most poignant feeling at this point was my desire to experience the beautiful gift of motherhood. A gift the Lord gives to only women, a gift in which a man and woman come together, expressing their love, to procreate, resulting in a precious little miracle. A miracle is exactly what a sweet child is. God's creation, growing inside a mother who offers unconditional love unlike any other on the human level. This is the closest analogy we can make to God's love for each of us. And to think that women are the only ones equipped to carry this special gift!

I prayed during this time that someday God would answer my prayers and provide me a God-fearing husband who would not just help create such a miracle but also help raise this little miracle with me. I literally have had glimpses of myself holding this beautiful child in my arms; kissing the smooth, squishy skin; listening to the tiny breaths; smelling the scents only an infant gives to the world (I'm not talking just the stinky ones); and admiring this helpless little being given to me and my husband to raise in this broken world and instill the little one with a strong, powerful belief in God. This is the vision I still have today, and I know God will provide if that is a part of His plan. However, the waiting and uncertainty are far from easy. No matter what, though, I choose to believe that God is the One and Only, who has my best interests in mind, according to His timing.

We hear the following throughout our lives:

"Timing is everything."
"It will happen at the right time."
"Only time will tell."
"It's all in God's timing."

Yes to all these statements. I believe in the truth of all of them, but I know I am not alone when I say that I wish I could have a glimpse into that divine timing, into where my life will end up, who my partner will be, the trials and triumphs I will experience along the rest of the way, and the growth that will happen in between!

Time—

It's precious.

It goes fast.

It waits for no one.

But it's all worth it!

We just need to be patient, which is so challenging for our minds, hearts, and souls!

God knows all our thoughts, questions, desires, hurts, weariness, and jealous moments. He wants us to take them all to Him. Journaling has always helped me process whatever I am going through. It also reminds me that it's okay to feel the feelings and to let go of my illusion of control because I'm not the one in control—God is.

As I began to slowly let go of control, I also began crossing paths with several guys with whom I'd had contact from late May to early August. I believe that everyone we meet can teach us something. Sometimes that something hurts. Sometimes that something ends up being a broken heart. Sometimes that something entails our realizing more of what you we've been looking for and how far we have come. Each one of the guys I met in those two and a half months taught me something.

Bachelor #1—Lesson Learned: *It's important not to lead someone on.*

There wasn't an attraction, or even much of an interest, on my end. Yes, he was someone to text and chat with, but at my age I knew I didn't want to waste either of our time.

Bachelor #2—Lesson Learned: *Lack of motivation is not attractive.*

I met the masked waiter at a wine bar where two of my college friends and I had gone one night. A total classic college move of writing my number on the receipt led him to text me. We texted back and forth for a while, but the lack of motivation and action to meet up wasn't there on his part. I could have kept chatting and reaching out to him, but to do so would not have solidified the boundaries I wanted to have.

Bachelor #3—Lesson Learned: *Stay true to yourself.*

I met a man while watching my mom play pickleball at one of her tournaments. We chatted, and I enjoyed the conversation. He was easy to talk to, active, and outgoing. He asked for my number and ended up texting and asking if he could take me out to dinner. I told him yes but was unsure of when. I later was honest and told him I was feeling more of a friendship vibe. Although this connection didn't end up going anywhere, I held true to who I was and was up front and honest.

During these months I watched Gabrielle Stone's live podcast interview with a self-aware narcissist. Gabrielle Stone is the bestselling author of *Eat, Pray, #FML*, which I referred to earlier. In her book Gabrielle shares that she found out her husband was cheating on her and that he was a narcissist. She divorced him, fell in love with another man, and was about to go to Europe with him when he dumped her right before getting onto the plane.

Although she was heartbroken, she decided to follow through with a solo adventure, just as Elizabeth Gilbert reported doing in *Eat, Pray, Love*. That adventure changed her life! While listening to the live interview, I had so many questions to ask the self-aware narcissist she was interviewing. My heart started racing as I listened. To discover five years after Scammer that my body still reacted this way was wild.

Trauma brings triggers. And triggers will always be a part of me. Through the work I have done, I can acknowledge the triggers and the trauma I've experienced, and I can allow myself to sit; cry, if needed; and feel. As I listened to the conversation, those were exactly my responses. It was an interesting conversation that brought up dormant feelings I had to process. Not only feelings about Scammer, but also feelings about starting the summer without a boyfriend for the first time in a few years.

Despite knowing that I was right where I was supposed to be in my journey, I still had feelings about the one-year anniversary of being single coming up in August, feelings about being alone and even being forgotten.

In this emotional moment, I came across an ad for *Zoosk*, an online dating website. As those sites tend to do, it hooked me. While searching the site, I noticed a man's smile, read his profile, and concluded that he seemed like an all-around good guy. (Let's be real, though; how does anyone really know from so little information?) I went back and forth about whether to get a subscription, because these sites hook you with "looking" for free. Then, if you want to read or send any messages, *bam*! They want your money! This man with the genuine smile messaged me. So, I caved and purchased a subscription to see what he had written.

"Hi."

That's all?! What?! I paid for a month's subscription for that?

Well, I messaged him back, along with a couple of others because, let's face it, that's what you do when you online date. My gut was reminding me of what I had told myself after Scammer: that I would never go back onto a dating website. However, when I saw Bachelor #4's smile and read a little more about him, I was interested. Never say never, I guess.

Bachelor #4—Lesson Learned: *Embrace the spontaneous moments!*

We messaged back and forth for a bit before exchanging numbers. Then he called! He actually called, not texted. I, of course, didn't answer because I don't answer numbers I don't recognize (ha!), but he left a message. I prayed first and then called him back. He suggested we meet for coffee. "Like *now*?" I asked him.

Yup, that's exactly what he meant! Coffee and conversation turned into grabbing a bite to eat and a drink, followed by another drink downtown, which led to a walk, during which he unexpectedly grabbed my hand and held onto it. A surge of butterflies and energy went through me. I didn't know if it was the alcohol in my system or the thrill of possibility, but I embraced the moment and kept walking as we stopped for one last drink at another bar. He drove me back to my car; we hugged; and he gave me a quick, unexpected kiss and then texted to make sure I got home safely, which I appreciated.

The next day I didn't hear from him much. He did tell me he was going out on Lake Michigan with some friends. At one point he asked whether his messages were getting through, which they hadn't been, but to know he was at least trying to reach out and share his day with me was a welcome feeling. A photo of him on his boat with friends came through at one point. And then nothing. When I say nothing, I mean *nothing*—up until this very day! Who knows what happened? I guess you could say I was ghosted. Happens to the best of us, I suppose!

When I reflect on this encounter, I am reminded that there's always a reason you meet someone and that you learn something from each dating experience, whether it's one date or two years of dating.

Bachelor #4 had brought out spontaneity in me that I always carry deep inside but don't always show. From talking to him on the phone to spending the next nine hours together, I felt God telling me, "Go! Why not?" And I did! I took the hours as they came, and it was so much fun! Who cares if I never heard from him again? I'd had a fun summer night out! One that reminded me of the free and spontaneous pieces of me deep within that I need and want to bring out more often. So, when a call comes in, take it! And then throw on a pair of jeans and a T-shirt and go, have some fun!

With the five-year anniversary of what I had renamed my Freedom Day quickly approaching, I decided to schedule a session with Michelle. The main takeaways included:

» Her encouraging me to read *The Body Keeps Score* by Bessel Van Der Kolk, a book about how the body is affected by trauma and the layers of trauma that tend to build up within.
» My timeline of the past five years. There were realizations that occurred while Michelle drew this out for me . . .
    - 6/29/16: First session with Michelle
    - 2 years: Dated Greg
    - 2 years: Dated Jay
    - 1 year (and counting): Single

After the session I took time to reflect. My long ago first session with Michelle had exposed the top of my trauma tree, which had involved almost seven years of my life with the "king" of masquerades, followed by two other guys who had also masked themselves and were inauthentic. Each was leading me to where I am now . . . and to figuring out who it is I really am. It hit me that I had spent four out of five years since then in relationships and, prior to that, seven years communicating back and forth with a narcissist.

It became clear in this session that I need a partner who understands trauma. A partner who understands that triggers and traumas will always be part of me. There will be times I will be triggered, yes, but I want the person God puts into my life to hold me, love me, and understand what trauma has done, knowing at the same time that the moment won't last. I need someone to acknowledge the trauma, knowing they can't fix it, but being there all the same to comfort and love me to get through these moments. When Michelle coached me through this, it was a huge ah-ha moment! It put words to my feelings, emotions, needs, and wants.

The next day I took a walk and listened to Cory Asbury's song "Dear God." The lyrics were about questioning and struggling with love, and through these moments the faith and trust to keep trying to love again. I felt as though God were speaking directly to me and telling me that I *will* love again. I have found that music speaks to me when I seem to need it most. In this moment I felt God's presence and the hope that I would love again, not knowing what that might look like or who might receive that love but acknowledging that I have a whole lot of love to give.

All through this past season of dating—through the ups and downs, the hills and valleys, and the multiple roller coasters—I knew that my love had always been there! It might have gotten deflated, beaten down, or been smacked around every once in awhile, but it hadn't gone anywhere!

In the moments when it seemed as though I weren't enough, little did I know that God was building up my store of love. He was preparing me for what was to come, . . . and He still is. He will continue to do so, not just for me but for you as well! I prayed that God would continue to guide me as I navigated online dating yet again. I prayed for discernment about who was safe and the ability to quiet the noise surrounding me in order to hear God's voice clearly. I prayed for God to guard my heart, but to also keep it open to love again.

Bachelor #5—Lesson Learned: Don't force it. If you know, you know.

I connected with Bachelor #5 on Facebook Dating. We met for a drink one afternoon, but I just wasn't feeling it. You might be thinking, *Stacey, it was one drink! Give the poor guy a chance!* I was starting to slowly learn to pay attention to my gut ahead of time and don't want to waste anyone else's time when it is speaking. I went home and texted him that I thought he was a nice guy but just didn't see anything happening other than our being friends. I have learned, and am still learning, that this is okay! Why lead each other on when you know from the get-go that it probably won't go anywhere?

Bachelor #6—Lesson Learned: Recognize and break unhealthy patterns.

I connected with yet another guy on Zoosk. We had been messaging back and forth, eventually exchanging numbers. He called and we talked for a while. I remember thinking, *Why am I always drawn to the guys I probably shouldn't be drawn to?* Bachelor #6 lived in a smaller town two or so hours away. He was divorced and had a son in high school. He seemed to be that "bad boy" type that you want to know more about. I remember thinking this after one of our conversations, during which he told me about all the "crazy" girls he had been talking to online.

He wanted to know my story, so I shared it. He was pretty taken aback by it all and didn't really seem to understand. I remember hanging up and feeling my gut kicking in again, but also hearing Sally, the name I've given to my inner critic, saying, *Oh, come on! How can he truly understand your story? It probably does seem pretty wild!*

Well, sure, but that doesn't mean I should ever feel as though I should hide that part of me. It is, after all, a story of redemption, of healing, of resilience, and of growth. I should never feel as though someone is shaming me for what I've gone through. I've learned that I've already shamed myself enough in the past. Bachelor #6 and I continued to text and talk on the phone. At one point we FaceTimed. I had felt like I was trying to defend myself after sharing my story, and feelings of shame were creeping back up to the surface. One day I ended up being late for a tutoring session because I was talking to this guy on the phone, who made me feel like shit. Red Flag! The difference this time was that I knew the feeling and named it right away!

During this time I was reading *The Gifts of Imperfection* by Brené Brown. She writes about shame resilience. The steps of which are:

1. Name it.
2. Talk about it.
3. Own your story.
4. Tell the story.

It took time to figure out that the feelings Bachelor #6 was bringing up in me weren't good. I was talking to him and making sure (trying to make sure, at least) that he knew I was a good person—that I was good enough. How did my body feel? Scared. Triggered. Trying to retreat and not to spiral. Once I had prayed and really thought about it all, I realized that he was shaming me—or, rather, bringing to the surface the shame I had worked on releasing for years! I don't want anyone in my life who brings those feelings out.

I felt like a drowning puppy trying hard to paddle to the surface, longing for someone to see and accept me. My story is my own, and I am proud of that story. I have overcome a lot, and I need and want someone to see and acknowledge that, not to question me and label me substandard. I realized at that moment that *he wasn't good enough for me*! I felt proud of myself for being able to recognize this, being able to turn inward to continue to protect the little girl and the young adult from harm. I remember telling myself, *I love you, Stacey. You are safe, loved, and protected.* This was a huge turning point for me in recognizing the post-traumatic growth I'd made to get to this place!

We all have dating stories to share. Whether you've dated a little or a lot, what are some of the lessons you've learned along the way? How have you grown as an individual in discovering what you need and want in a relationship?

chapter 14

Discover, Forgive, and Comfort Your Inner Child

IN JULY, WHEN I spent time at my parents' house on the lake, I decided to organize some of my childhood boxes in the attic. I came across a bag full of letters I had written to my mom when I was growing up. I brought them down and started going through them with her. As I was reading them out loud, my inner child came out and I realized, thirty-one years later, that I had always been afraid of my mom leaving me, internalizing as a young child the possibility of losing her.

During the first five years of my life, my mom was diagnosed with stomach cancer, went through chemotherapy, and had major back surgery, all while raising two young children. I was scared whenever she left for business trips and worried when I spent a week with my grandparents each summer. I felt as though I had to tell her every little wrong thing I had done and the choices I had made because I didn't want her to leave me.

As I reflected on this while sitting with her at the patio table, tears were streaming down both of our faces, and I realized that some of my anxiety stems from fearing that people will leave. My mom had always told me that I was like her little nurse and that I had grown up more quickly than other kids. I have always been more mature for my age than many of my peers and have never liked being too far away from my mom. Even now, I worry if I don't hear from her.

It has always been hard for me to let people go or to cope with people leaving without my fully knowing why. I was so afraid of losing my mom at such a young age that I had internalized that fear more than I'd ever realized. As we sat there crying together, I grabbed her hand and reflected, "There wasn't anything we could have controlled. There is not a day goes by that I'm not incredibly thankful that God saved your life. That you were able to raise me and watch my beautiful life bloom and grow into the woman I am today!"

The next morning I finally took on one of the homework assignments Michelle had been encouraging me to do for quite some time. I wrote a letter to my little girl self:

> *Little Stacey,*
>
> I release you from all the grown-up things and feelings you felt when you were just a little girl. I acknowledge and am aware that even at a young age you were faced with some trauma that you have truly never brought to the surface until now. Mom is safe. She beat the cancer and is almost 31 years (and counting) in remission. She has seen you grow into a beautiful woman who is still working through a lot but continues to put in the work to recognize the hurt you've endured and to deal with the guilt and shame you've held onto for so many years.
>
> You, little Stacey, are good enough.
>
> You, little Stacey, are worthy enough.
>
> You, little Stacey, can let go of all you've spent so many years hiding and your uncertainty about how to express your emotions and just be a kid. Be free from the worry, anxiety, and mistakes you have faced and made along the way.

Give yourself the compassion you deserve and the kindness, love, and grace to yourself that you give to all those around you. You are loved, little Stacey, more than you ever know. Spread your wings and fly, my sweet inner child girl, and know I will always be here to protect, guide, support, forgive, and love you, no matter what.

You don't have to be so strong or independent or even feel like you must do it all. Let go. Be free. Live the life you were born to live! No matter what happens, I am just a whisper away to remind you of every bit of life and love you will face and endure, and of how much grace you have to give yourself through the whole process to overcome it all.

You, little Stacey, grew up to have such a resilient heart, not letting anything or anyone get in your way. You grew up to have the love and determination to keep going. You came to find out that you've always had this resilience, even as a little girl.

I love you!

Your Older Self,

Stacey

A few days later I drove home. That Sunday the church sermon was about what we crave or chase in this world rather than fully trusting God. It got me thinking, *What am I chasing*? I wrote the following in my journal:

Even though I didn't want to admit it, deep down I was chasing a relationship with a man. The chase was for a man to journey life with and to experience God's goodness and beauty with. A man who has similar morals, values, appreciation, and love for life. A man who understands relationships and how they take time to grow and develop and are ever changing. However, they are all based on a foundation.

For me, that foundation has to be God. Maybe others view spirituality—the connection with a higher power—differently from me. For me, that's God the Father, Jesus the Son, and the Holy Spirit. I truly believe this because I am a witness to His saving grace. At this moment I am declaring my desire to grow with the Lord in our relationship together. I pray that anyone He puts into my life to have any type of relationship with, romantic or friendship, will know where my spiritual foundation is found . . . in Jesus! With outstretched arms, I pray to stop craving and start trusting!

My security rests in the Lord. I pray that He will remind me of all I have, of the gratefulness I feel, and of the love I share, molding me to be more like Him every single day. I thank God for this life He has given me—for the trials and triumphs I've been through . . . and for the ones still ahead.

Shortly after journaling, I sat down at my computer to continue to write. As I sat, staring at an empty screen, the following flowed from me to the keyboard and onto a document:

July 11, 2021

It has hit me. In this exact moment, in this safe space at my dining room table, with cleansing tears streaming down my cheeks, I realize how the past sixteen months have affected my mind, body, soul, and spirit. It has hit me how my mind seemed to push down, block out, and tunnel into survival mode. My body tensed up, got beat up and thrown down, and I expected it to function normally without any rest or recovery time as it went into protective mode, not just for itself, but for the 24 six- and seven-year-olds who were under my watch, love, and care for eight hours each day, five days a week, for 180 days.

My soul was crushed from not always being listened to the first time, being taken for granted, and suffering deep down when I put on a protective shield as I listened to my colleagues and friends and to outsiders. My spirituality grew as I became closer to God because, honestly, He was the only One who was always there as I tried to figure out what was happening, where to go, what to do, whom to trust, and where my voice would be heard, wondering all the time why and how we were experiencing, and surviving, this pandemic.

At this moment, I broke.

My mind, body, soul, and spirit have all come together to embrace me in a long hug and tell me it's okay. It's okay to cry. It's okay to doubt. It's okay to let it all go, knowing that for the past sixteen months I have tried to be strong. This summer feels different. This summer feels weird. This summer is one I will always remember because it's when I finally began to work on my self-love, self-compassion, and self-acceptance. More importantly, it's the summer I realized it's okay to feel the pain, the hurt, the avoidance, and the numbness.

My body has been getting beat up for years. In May the trauma that had built up collapsed me in a burning, numbing pain down my left arm. Little did I know that this was my body talking to me, telling me it couldn't take much more and that it was time for me to listen. To stop feeling I had to save the world, or at least the people around me, not recognizing that I was neglecting myself in the process. When babies are neglected, they lose their sense of connection to human touch and love. No matter how old we are, if we neglect the most important human person, we lose our connection to and love for others because we don't have it for ourselves.

My mind is always in overdrive, and that can truly be dangerous. I've been working on this issue for years, using the techniques of thought stopping, reframing my thoughts, and talking to my inner critic to find the worthiness and identifying pieces of myself that I know *are* good enough to not just survive but thrive! This hasn't been easy, and, if I'm completely honest, it never will be. The mind is a powerful thing.

For the past sixteen months my mind has been numbed by endless scrolling on Instagram and Facebook in an effort to sabotage my thought process, to avoid disciplining myself to find and write the necessary words to get them out of my mind and onto paper. I would lie on my couch, thinking, *I could totally be writing right now and not scrolling.* But then Sally and my self-doubt would counteract with, *Well, what if people judge you on what you write? What if it's not good enough? What if it's not perfect? What if it ruins your career? What if you let everything out and then don't feel protected, secure, wanted?*

Who cares, anyway? We live our lives in fear of the what ifs rather than making vulnerability a norm. There shouldn't ever be a question beginning with "What if" in anyone's mind, but rather a thought, statement, or idea ending with "Why not?" or "What's stopping you?" and followed by a "Just do it!"

I want to write and publish a book telling my story. Why not? What's stopping me? *Just do it!*

I want to travel solo to places I've never been. Why not? What's stopping you? *Just do it!*

I want to experience love in which I don't have to wonder about my worth or whether I'm good enough for him. Why not? What's stopping you? *Just do it!*

This is the kind of thinking we should be doing, embracing, and believing in! Why not? What's stopping you? *Just do it!*

This kind of thinking is a process and always will be. When we reframe our thoughts to reflect, believe, and embrace the process, that is when our best living will take place!

My soul is pure.

My soul is full of feelings, emotions, and empathy.

My soul is fragile.

My soul believes the best in others.

My soul is a protector of others.

My soul has been hurt many times.

My soul is broken but continues to be put back together, piece by piece.

My soul loves God and others but most of the time forgets to love herself.

My soul has been crushed without realizing it these past sixteen months, and this summer is the time to rebuild it.

This will take time and will not be easy. It's crazy how one blow to your soul can shatter it into a million pieces and how it takes days, months, and sometimes years to rebuild. We want to protect our souls at all costs and not let others in. Our subconscious knows the damage that can be done and the amount of time it will need to rebuild. This is where I am now: rebuilding my soul, establishing boundaries to do so, and showing myself the love and self-compassion I deserve.

My spiritual journey has been in progress for the past 14 years (and counting). These past 16 months have brought a whole new level to my journey. After growing up Catholic and moving away from that tradition as I sought more spiritually, I found the missing piece in a relationship with Jesus. After parting ways with Jay, I came to realize that thc only One who will never let me down is God.

While reading through my journal collection to prepare for writing this book, I was reminded how change took place when I turned inward to my spiritual, God-loved and God-breathed self. I could feel the increased level of intimacy and relationship through the almost endless number of prayers I have written. My entries turned into talking to God rather than feeling I'm alone and have to figure things out on my own.

These past months I have experienced what Brené Brown refers to as many "spiritual awakening moments." All these moments have brought me closer to God, my surroundings, and my own brokenness, resulting in continued healing. There hasn't just been my inner trauma, but also the massive amounts of trauma to our country and this world as we live through a pandemic.

Trying to piece it all together isn't worth the fight; the exhaustion; the hurt; and the endless asking whether I am doing enough, being enough, doing my part, etc. We all have our views about religion and spirituality. My job is to love, not to judge anyone else for what they believe, what they do, how they see themselves, . . . and the list goes on. My job is to show the love that God shows us and gives to me daily. My job is not to judge—and neither is yours (Matthew 7:1–6).

I dove into rereading my journals, tagging the moments I knew I wanted to include, and continued to write my book. While I was rereading the journals about Greg, I reflected on the beginning of that relationship. How easy it had seemed to be. However, as I reread, I realized that Greg had still been in therapy with his ex when we met.

I don't think the couple had even broken up yet. I reread the part at which I came back from a weekend away and he told me that he and his ex-girlfriend had been talking and that she wanted to try things again.

I look back now and realize that I should have said "See ya!" However, I wanted to be "fought for," desired, the one he would end up choosing. I see now that I was hoping for a movie ending. I've learned and now know that I deserve and desire better! Three different times he did this to me. Three! Until enough really was enough! Looking back, I see that I was part of the problem by hoping each time that he would come back and choose me. I also see my own growth and am giving myself grace and compassion I couldn't see or give to myself back then.

PAUSE AND REFLECT

How many of you are like me and give freely to others all. of. the. time? Do you find yourself getting hurt by being true to yourself? Do you start asking yourself, How and why does this keep happening to me? *Take a minute to think or journal about these times. When you're done, think about where you are right now.*

- Are you the same person today as you were when those hurtful things happened?
- Would you consider yourself a better, stronger person now because of or despite those things?

Michelle reminds me about *The Four Agreements*, written by Don Miguel Ruiz. Agreement #1 is "Be impeccable with your word." Agreement #2 is "Don't take anything personally." I often have to remind myself that not everything is about me! We can remain compassionate and kind to others while still protecting ourselves, which is part of boundary work.

Boundary setting is tough, it's hard, and it takes a lot of effort and time. But it's worth it! As I reflect on the journey I'm on regarding boundaries, which honestly has just begun, let me tell you from experience that boundaries are not always welcomed by others. However, that's all part of the work. When you do this work and let go, this is when you find yourself growing and blooming more and more!

One Saturday I experienced a God-driven, God-felt, God-loved type of morning as I walked into a local cosmetic shop to receive a facial I had won. I cannot describe the experience Rachel Williams, the owner, provided, but I know that she offered a God-given gift to my face. My soul was filled with peace, motivation, and love!

Afterward, as I walked out, I was greeted with a smile by Rachel. The floodgates burst open! My face not only felt alive, but I felt alive! Releasing our inner beauty and seeing and feeling what God sees in us is unexplainable. Rachel's words, prayers, and conversation that day were precisely what I had needed at that moment of my journey. Before I left, she prayed that all the doubt-filled, Satan-driven thoughts would be pushed out of my mind because there was and still is absolutely no place for them!

Releasing our inner beauty and seeing and feeling what God sees in us is unexplainable.

Toward the beginning of her prayer, she used the word *unlock*. She prayed that I would allow myself to unlock my words, so they could flow freely as I continued to write my story. It was becoming clear that I was unlocking love for myself in this process.

Two nights before taking the Lake Michigan shoreline adventure I've always wanted to take, I went out for a couple of drinks. A good friend told me that one of the workers at a local bar was super cute and seemed so nice. Whenever she talked to him, she said she always thought about me. So, why not? Time to check him out for myself!

I got to the Holiday Bar, ordered a drink, and stood outside listening to the live music. I was texting my friend and taking photos of one of the waiters to see whether he was the one she was referring to, when, all of a sudden, he passed by, and I knew it was him. I stood outside for a little longer and was even asked to join a group of girls for whom I had just taken a group photo. I politely turned down their invitation because I was in a chill mood and didn't feel like mingling. I went back inside, found a seat at the bar, and began talking with the bartender. At one point I remember a guy passing by, telling one of the bartenders he had to go do something. Some time passed, and the bar started to get busier.

Suddenly, the same guy who had left was back and asked to sit next to me. We spent the next two hours or so chatting. He shared about his two boys, what he likes to do, about his past, and about his family. I remember thinking that he seemed to have the most genuine, kindest heart. He walked me to my car, gave me a hug, and then texted me later to make sure I had gotten home safely. He suggested meeting for coffee the next day and even mentioned a couple of places. One of his texts said, "Whatever works. Having the chance to interact and see you is what I desire." After reading his response, I thought to myself, *Um, excuse me? Is this a man leading?*

The next morning we texted some more, and Vince seemed like a man with a good head on his shoulders. When talking to Vince, I was reminded that I feel there is something to be said for men who have children. If they are an involved parent, which Vince seemed to be, they have to support, love, and keep their children healthy and alive. It was clear that Vince loves his boys and has so much fun with them! They are two lucky little humans to have him as their father!

The one thing I was hesitant about was his sharing that he couldn't have any more children. Although I'm open to being a bonus mom, I also want to try to have at least one child of my own someday, God willing. I prayed but also felt in my gut that I didn't want to lead him on.

Vince and I met for a walk at a local park the next day. I was glad we were able to meet before I left on my solo adventure. Although he seemed like a humble, sweet man, I kept feeling that I wanted to be free from anyone and anything that might distract me from this up-north adventure. So, I decided to create a boundary. I was going to shut off my phone and check in with people at night. I prayed to embrace each moment ahead!

PAUSE AND REFLECT

A lot of who we are, our behaviors, and what we think about ourselves stems from our inner child. When thinking about your childhood:

- What feelings surface?
- When did you feel the safest?
- What were you most afraid of?

Do these fears, feelings, and the way you view yourself today stem from how you felt as a child? If so:

- When do you feel these surfacing the most?
- What do you default to in order to protect yourself? Is this something you remember doing as a child that has carried into your adulthood?

When you are ready, I challenge you to write a letter to your inner child, your younger self. Let the words fall and tell your inner child all that you've been holding in. Let it go. Releasing it will hopefully produce comfort and, peace . . . and maybe even a stream of tears. Let them flow!

Embrace Every Moment

> "For I know the plans I have for you, declares the LORD, plans to prosper you and not to harm you, plans to give you hope and a future." Jeremiah 29:11 (NIV)

AT 9:00 A.M. I hopped into Turbo, my SUV, and off I went! I sped past a field of sunflowers, squealed, and initially kept driving. One thing to know about me is that I love sunflowers, so to see a whole field of them was amazing! I had driven a little farther when I felt my gut saying, *What are you doing? Turn around!* That's exactly what I did! I turned around, parked on the side of the street, got out, and took several photos of the beauty in front of me. I walked across the street to get a closer look. The amazing thing was that all the sunflowers were facing the sun. These beautiful flowers were looking toward their light source to get fed.

How often do we wander aimlessly, when all we have to do is look up to see our Light Source full of unconditional love, forgiveness, hope, and grace? The Light Source gives us the strength, the focus to stand tall in our thoughts, actions, values, and beliefs. To share and show love that can only come from One Source—Jesus! No wonder sunflowers are one of my favorite flowers! This was certainly a reminder to slow down, turn around, and look at what was right in front of me.

After my stop at the sunflowers, I drove to Pierport, a small lookout with only a taste of the blue I was about to witness in the stops ahead.

Next stop, Arcadia. I stopped at the overlook, but it didn't do justice to what I was about to see when hiking Baldy Dune! I took the longer route by walking the trails. To walk and hear the different sounds, especially the rain from the night before still dripping from the trees, was a wonderful, calming experience. I reflected on the time two years earlier when I had been hiking with Jay, walking behind him and thinking that this was the man I wanted to spend my life with. We all know how that ended up, and the reality was that I couldn't have been happier at that moment to be hiking by myself. I embraced this hike, found a sandy nook I claimed as my own and wrote a poem.

My Little Nook

Arcadia Bluff—Baldy Dune

Find a nook—take it
The view is incredible
The water's color, indescribable
A seagull with the best bird's-eye view anyone could imagine.
There is no sound as calming as crashing waves coming in to
the shore.
The sun, brightly shining above
Me, in my own little nook
away from the hustle and bustle, the noise of this world
Recentering on what truly matters:
My breath
My soul within

The clarity I seek . . . yearn for
The wind blows
just like my memories
one way and then the other
When will they calm down?
They will never go away
because just like the wind
they slow down,
But they will always blow in and out
slightly—
    This is what makes a memory.

This moment in time is a new memory I'm making for myself
One I hope to be brought back to—
the calm
When I feel life speeding up
or when I feel like I'm losing control

This moment
This memory
This place
My little nook.

After spending time in my little nook, I decided to walk halfway down the dune before walking back up and back to my car. At that moment I felt a little lighter.

Next up, Frankfort! What a cute little town. I found the local brewery, Stormcloud, ordered a flight of beer and a BLT pizza, and had a nice conversation with an older man who reminded me of my dad. This encounter reminded me of the people you meet along the way, which is always a part of traveling for me.

Shortly afterward, I made my way to Point Betsie Lighthouse and took the tour. It was fun to hear a ten-minute history of the lighthouse and then head up the winding staircase to its top. As I descended, I looked out the little window onto the clearest water. I told the guide, "I can't believe the water looks like this in Michigan, . . . and to think we get to live here!" It looked like the waters in the Caribbean. I was in awe and spent time taking in the crystal blue water and the crashing waves before heading on to Empire.

I found a hiking trail that led to a beach with one small group of people further down the shore and no one else . . . but literally millions of little rocks. Breathtaking! The rocks were so smooth from traveling along the sand, waves, and water. I was able to set up my phone and capture a classic jumping-in-the-air photo or two before leaving! On the walk back to the car, it was just me and the soothing sounds of nature as I prayed for clarity regarding men, for whatever it was He has planned for me, and for me to embrace His vision for my life. In that moment I could feel the Lord working in me as I breathed in and kept repeating, "Quiet mind . . . Quiet soul."

After my stop at Empire, I made my way to my bed and breakfast, Sylvan Inn in Glen Arbor. I was surprised at how big the inn was and immediately loved the cuteness of my room. I showered and rested a bit before heading to Cherry Republic for a peaceful dinner, after which I took a walk around the small town and headed to the beach just in time for the sunset.

As I was sitting there, a ladybug appeared on my towel. It was moving slowly and clung to me once I picked it up. It looked as though it wasn't going to last much longer. This was the first of my ladybug encounters on this trip.

I loved sitting there and watching the sun change colors as it set. Sunsets are one of my favorite sights. I ended the day with such a peaceful mindset, new memories replacing those from the last time I had been in Glen Arbor with Greg, and the freedom of knowing that I had completely allowed the day to unfold in the way it was meant to.

The next morning, I woke up thinking I might hike Sleeping Bear Dunes. However, after hiking Arcadia the day before, my body just wasn't feeling it. So, I listened to my body and decided to go with the flow of whatever the day brought.

I started with breakfast at the inn, while journaling and texting two close friends. Little did I know that I needed to talk with both. One brought up a great point about feeling as though, as you get older, it's hard to find or be interested in someone with whom you are equally yoked—that is, someone who thinks the same way you do about faith and other matters of importance (2 Corinthians 6:14–18). At this time, I was just feeling in my gut that I couldn't lead Vince on. I was trying to listen to my gut more and more deliberately; as my friend, who has known me since the sixth grade, mentioned, this was the time to reflect and pray, to be still in it all.

I finished my breakfast and, on my way out of town, stopped at the M-22 store. I decided to collect stickers from each stop on this trip. As I was buying my sticker, my phone went off. There was Miles's name looking back at me! There had been multiple conversations from January on up to this point, and I found myself holding onto hope about him—which was a huge reason I had prayed for clarity the day before in the woods.

His message read, "Hey Stace. Thanks for the message. Listen, I think you're a great woman. Unfortunately, I think my home base is here for now, and I would like to date younger. You will be such a good partner and mother someday. There's just too much I need to figure out in terms of whether I want kids, as well as with my faith. I don't want to waste your time. Maybe our paths will cross in the future. I hope you have a nice rest of the summer and school year."

My response was simply: "Thanks for letting me know. Wishing you well and hope you enjoy the rest of your summer!"

I didn't have a plan at this point, so I just drove. I reflected on Miles's message and remembered the start to my trip—being so frustrated, hurt, and uncertain and crying out to God to give me peace while tears streamed down my cheeks. Well, this was definitely the clarity I needed, and I was grateful it had come near the beginning of the trip!

I passed the Snowbird Inn, where I would be staying for the next few nights, and then saw a sign for Green Bird Cellars. I drove past, but something was telling me to go back. I did, and found that it was a beautiful winery—but it was closed. I told myself I would be back!

From there I made my way into Northport and decided to park and walk around. I went to the marina, where I thought a lot about Vince and what I felt I needed to do. While praying about it, I stopped at a few stores. I bought several cards at one store, all written and illustrated by the same author/artist; the women on the front of each card reminded me of myself. I bought them with the plan to write cards to myself, reminding me not to lose heart in who I am . . . ever!

Afterward, I bought a coffee at the New Bohemian Café and ordered a sandwich. I decided to change into my swimsuit, buy a beer at the gas station, and head to Christmas Cove Beach to enjoy lunch there. As I waited for my sandwich, I was writing in my journal when a construction worker, who must have been on his lunch break, walked by and said, "I hope it has a happy ending!" The timing of his saying this—knowing as I did that I was writing my book and enjoying my solo adventure—brought me a whisper of comfort. This is when I knew in my heart that a record of these days would be the culminating chapters of my book.

When I arrived at Christmas Cove Beach, it was like Christmas in Ju . . . August! There weren't a lot of people there yet, so I grabbed an open spot and laid out my stuff. As I ate, drank, and read, I breathed in the scene. Yet someone was still on my mind: Vince. As I walked into the turquoise blue water of Lake Michigan and submerged myself into the cold oasis, I prayed out loud, yet again, for clarity.

Sometimes it takes sitting in fifty-degree water to think and see clearly. In those moments I felt the needed clarity come to me. I was just interested in being friends with Vince, and my gut supported this. I felt better after getting out of the water and reflecting on similar feelings I'd had when Jay and I had gone to the farmer's market and then gone back to his place to fix lunch. My gut had been trying to tell me something on that day, but I hadn't listened.

There was no doubt that Vince and I would have fun times together, but I didn't want to go through another relationship with something not feeling right. I knew what I needed to do. The night before I had typed out a draft of a message I wanted to send him. I pulled it up then and pushed *Send*. I didn't want to look at my phone for a while afterward to see the way he would respond, but I prayed he would understand.

This trip was helping me realize how important it is to have self-love and be comfortable being single, experiencing what life and this world have to offer. I didn't want to feel any additional pressure to date. I knew I was in a happy place in my life, and I thanked God for that!

After Christmas Cove Beach, I went back to Green Bird Cellars, where I was able to write, taste wine, and explore the vineyard. As I walked, I viewed ahead of me a field of beautiful purple lavender! There was a man toward the top of the hill who shouted down to me that this was private property. I apologized, but then he said, "Feel free to take a photo. I won't tell the owner!" Come to find out, he was the owner! He used to own Green Bird Cellars but had sold the land, keeping this part of it. Talking to Stan was a blessing!

Our paths were meant to cross. He shared about the charity work he does to help people get back on their feet, find a job, and acquire the necessary skills, socially and professionally, to make a living. As Stan said, "I believe we have to start working individually, one-on-one with people. It only takes one person to make a world of difference!"

Our conversation gave me hope for the beautiful humanity surrounding us. As I walked back down the hill to the winery, I thought to myself, *The people you meet along the way on this journey of life are truly little God winks.* I was discovering that the key to these moments is to be open to whatever and whomever may cross your path.

I left the winery and drove to Snowbird Inn, where I was greeted warmly by Alice. As I opened the door to my room, tears started to well. It was absolutely beautiful and matched exactly the way I felt—content, peaceful, light, and loved. My heart was so full! I ended the day taking in another breathtaking sunset on the beach in Leland. Deep gratitude filled my soul as I lay my head on the pillow and fell soundly asleep.

The next day, on my drive around the Leelanau Peninsula, I stopped at Peterson Park. I walked down the stairs, where I was greeted by a rock that read "Where's the Beach?" As I turned the corner, I understood what the message on that rock meant! This was not a sand beach but instead a rock beach, covered in rocks of all different shapes, sizes, textures, and colors, as far as the eye could see.

As I walked down the shore, all I could think about were the millions of colorful rocks surrounding me. I spotted a rock that reminded me of a foot and then decided to start my own cairn (a pile of rocks created as a memorial or landmark). I found another rock that was flat and round, salt and pepper in color. I put it on top of the foot, planning to return after collecting more. As I continued down the shoreline, I came across a huge boulder with waves crashing around it. I set up the camera timer on my phone and tried to capture all that I was feeling!

One of my favorite photos from this shoot is of me facing the water, making the heart sign with my hands . . . blissful love.

With whom? Just myself along the endless blue water and among the plethora of rocks. No one could take this moment away from me as I stood strong and resilient, calm and at peace on top of that boulder!

Walking back with more rocks in my hands, I began searching for the two rocks I had found earlier. I wanted these to be the base of my cairn. However, I couldn't find them.

How often do we walk past someone or something and never turn around? I was determined to find those rocks! I turned around, eyes moving back and forth in search of those two distinct stones. There they were, the salt and pepper stone supported by the flatter, foot-shaped rock! Dumping the new rocks I had collected, I sat down like a little kid ready to build and create. It was like a puzzle, trying to put the "right" stone in place so the whole structure wouldn't collapse. I made a couple of different cairns before settling on the final creation. Finally, I searched for a little, colorful stone to place on top. I thought about how many layers it had taken to build this cairn. The slightest wind would knock it over, but the base, the foundation, would always be there, inviting a rebuild.

How often do we build up our layers, get them knocked down, and then simply walk away from the mess? Strength is about getting knocked down and yet being determined to rebuild, knowing it might take a while because you have to get to the root of the problem before you can put the colorful stone back on top.

However, once all is rebuilt, you have the added strength and resilience that serve as a reminder of how beautiful you have become in the process. There will be times when the colorful stone gets knocked off, but when you have a solid foundation in your faith, beliefs, values, and love for yourself, you know it will someday be back on top. It will shine brightly as you look back and remember what it took to get to this place in your life. All you need to do is put one foot in front of the other. Oh, the symbolism of my finding that first rock in the shape of a foot. The strength I was discovering in my many layers and through the rebuilding was . . . love!

After Peterson Park, I drove to the lighthouse on the tip of the peninsula. The beach was once again all rock! I took off my shoes and socks and walked to the water's edge. As I put my feet in, they touched all different types of rocks; some smooth, some sharp, and all different in colors, shapes, and sizes. My feet felt the stones as I noted how crystal clear the water was. Seeing the rocks at my feet so clearly made me think about life.

Even when you are careful, you will come upon a rock (or person or job or time in your life) that is uncomfortable, but the only way to make your way back is to be brave, apply lighter pressure, and return. After walking back in the discomfort, I lay down on a bed of rocks, which, surprisingly, was quite comfortable and even soothing! After lying there for a bit, I walked back to my car and drove away.

God knows what will be; it's all according to His timing.

The next stop was Leelanau Cellars. I drove through Omena, thinking that Leelanau Cellars was in Suttons Bay, but it wasn't. I turned around to drive back and then spied a colleague of mine walking in Suttons Bay! I honked, rolled down my window, and yelled, "Meg!" I pulled off the road and ran to say hello. She gave me one of the best hugs as we caught up a bit. If I hadn't thought Leelanau Cellars was in Suttons Bay, I wouldn't have encountered a friend! What were the odds? God's timing amazes me, and I have to remind myself of that often. God knows what will be; it's all according to His timing.

I did a tasting at Leelanau Cellars before ordering a Frosé with a wine topper and taking it outside to enjoy the view. Afterward, I took a stroll to Omena Beach before going back to The Knot for an M43 beverage, a salad, a view of the water, and the best background music. I started talking to a couple who had come with their two small kids and, yet again, felt the power of engaging in conversation with people I met along the way.

Back to Snowbird Inn to shower and take a quick nap before heading to the Cove for dinner. I sat outside, observing what was going on around me and enjoying the freshly caught whitefish. As I walked to the beach to catch the sunset, the sun slid behind the clouds. Some observers might have left then, but I decided to go anyway to write . . . and I'm so glad I did! The sky was beautifully pink and the water calm, and I was so happy I could experience this, even though it wasn't exactly what I had expected.

Isn't that how life is sometimes? Some things end up being better than expected. I felt this repeatedly on my solo adventure. Life is an amazing phenomenon, and I wanted to continue the ride!

I woke up the next morning feeling that today would be a great day to hike Sleeping Bear Dunes! I set off with my daypack and Nalgene of water, ready for the hike ahead. I remember visiting Sleeping Bear Dunes a few years earlier with a friend, but we had turned back because the clouds had grown dark and we didn't want to be caught on the dunes in a storm. Today I was determined to make it to the shoreline!

It was a gorgeous day, with the sun shining brightly and a slight breeze. I took in God's beauty along the way and enjoyed seeing people climbing the dunes, some turning back, some panting as they ascended yet another steep path, and hearing a lot of laughter. Once I reached Lake Michigan, I walked down the shoreline and found a secluded spot. I set up a little space for myself and then had the desire to take the plunge and go skinny dipping!

I had not done so before but had had this on my bucket list for years. I had always been afraid of letting others see my body, but now it was just me and the water, with no one else around. Until a man jogged by. I waited until he was far out of sight and hoped he wouldn't come back the same way. My gut said that it was now or never. As I contemplated whether to fully commit, I wrote a little pep talk to myself:

> Live in the moment.
> Show and give compassion to yourself, Stace!
> Feel the fresh water on your skin and the freedom being naked brings.
> Love the skin you're in.

You are beautiful, Stacey, not just on the outside, but in!
Be brave.
Be strong.
Be courageous!
You've got this!

I looked around, took off my sports bra and bathing suit bottoms, took a deep breath, and ran! I realized right away that the first several feet of lake bottom were completely covered with rock, but that didn't stop me. I plunged into the water and started to swim. The experience was sheer bliss! In those few moments I felt different from what I had ever felt before. This was a freedom and vulnerability that, this time, I had chosen for myself.

In that moment I felt that my body was beautiful and experienced a surge of love and compassion for myself. I felt myself infused with the strength to let go of fear, to abandon those thoughts of not being good enough, to override the years of body shaming. None of it mattered at that moment because it was just me, myself, and I!

If you can't be comfortable with yourself, how can you be comfortable with someone else? I've struggled with feeling good enough for a man because of the shame I had carried from my past for so long. After that moment of liberation, I looked to my left and saw the man running back my way. I had to make a choice: go back in or wait until he passed?

I chose to go back in.

Wrapping up in my sandy towel, I put on my bathing suit bottoms only and sat in the sand. I looked down and found a white rock shaped like a heart; it symbolized for me purity, love, and compassion—for myself. Once the runner had passed, I looked to my left again and saw two kayakers. I wanted to go back into the water, but they were headed my way. I chose to put on my sports bra, eat my Granny Smith apple, and feel the refreshing water on my feet.

I cannot describe what this moment meant to me—the instant I chose to face the fear of being vulnerable. This was one step forward in my intimate and sexual healing, and I was proud of the love and compassion I had shown for myself. I am grateful still for this experience and know that the timing was perfect! I saw myself as the Lord does: Free. Intimate. Whole. Loved. I am forever grateful for this moment of healing—though I know the journey will be unending.

I walked back to Turbo, drove back to the inn, showered, and was off to Hop Lot, where I relaxed and enjoyed some IPAs, dinner, and the superb atmosphere. The last call was announced, so I ordered another beer as I wrote in my journal. I decided to take a walk and noticed a woman sitting on a bench with a man, who, I learned, was just a friend. She commented on my fanny pack, and we talked for a bit before I continued on my way.

I had taken a seat by the fire, finishing my beer, when she came by. She told me that she and her fiancé had broken things off after having been together for seven years. She had decided to go on this trip anyway! We exchanged numbers, and I hoped to keep in touch as we traveled through life. On my drive back to the inn, I reflected on what a gift it is to meet other people while traveling. These unexpected encounters had begun in Savannah, continued in Scottsdale, and are still happening today.

When I returned to my room, I turned on the light and saw a second ladybug moving around on the lampshade. I was so thankful for another day to be alive and to be me!

PAUSE AND REFLECT

When you think about the moments that occur in your life, do you find yourself moving forward to embrace them, running away from them, or letting them pass you by?

- Recall a moment in your life you recall fully embracing?
- Think about a moment you found yourself running away from someone, something, a situation, etc.
- What memorable moment did you let pass by?
- Do you regret not embracing certain moments, having later discovered how much you wish you had?

It's never too late! Embrace every moment because they truly do come when they're meant to!

chapter 16

Unlocking Your True Self

THE NEXT DAY could be best described by the phrase "ebb and flow." But let me start by telling you that I'm an Enneagram One. Let me explain.

During the pandemic, I started reading and learning more about the Enneagram. One of my closest friends introduced me to it, and we have had many in-depth conversations about it. I go back to the Enneagram to help me put words to how I have felt most of my life. I was struggling in July 2020 when my friend sent me an excerpt from a book she was reading about Type One personalities and their inner child. Her response had me in tears: "I just want you to know you don't need to be any better. You *are* good enough, and I love you to pieces and always see your whole heart!"

I wrote the following reflection in my journal around this time.

> I've been struggling lately. I want to be in my healthy place. I know I will get there again, but I wish I could just stay there. Being

and becoming more aware of who I am makes me realize a lot may stem from how I viewed the world and myself as a little girl. Did I do the dishes correctly? Wash the car a certain way? Think about the errors/mistakes I made playing basketball rather than what had gone well in a game? Second guess something I said and being on edge about how others were going to react?

As a child, you aren't aware of this and how this mindset affects you, but as you get older and start living on your own, away from your parents, you slowly become more aware of what you held onto and developed from your childhood. Like the feeling of always having to be good enough, a hyper focus on doing your absolute best and not making mistakes, and the constant presence of a strong inner critic; all describe a Type One individual. I had always put enough pressure on myself, never feeling that I was good enough when in relationships with Scammer, Greg, Jay, or any other guys I went out on dates with. I always tried to compensate so they wouldn't get upset about something I said or did.

God has made me, and you, to be enough. To truly and wholeheartedly see ourselves as such, we have to forgive ourselves, accept ourselves fully, let go of whatever culture might say about us, and live into what God says about us!

I struggle because inside I don't want to do everything or be everything to everyone. I want to be loved and accepted fully for who I am. I don't always want to feel that I have to plan, pick up stuff, clean, and have everything in its place. That's exhausting. Part of me feels that a man won't want to be with me because there are moments when I don't want to micromanage. I don't want to be rigid, critical, or judgmental.

The funny thing is that the one person I tend to be the most rigid, critical, and judgmental toward is *me*! I want to release this tendency forever, knowing that, if I do that, I will not be who the Lord made me to be. God has made me, and you, to be enough. To truly and wholeheartedly see ourselves as such, we have to forgive ourselves, accept ourselves fully, let go of whatever culture might say about us, and live into what God says about us!

As I learned more about the Enneagram, I connected it to *The 5 Love Languages* by Gary Chapman. My top love language is Quality Time. Spending time and being present with my loved ones and friends and engaging in conversation with them fills me up. The reason Words of Affirmation constitutes my next top love language is that I don't always feel I am enough. I feel as though I could have done things better, said something more clearly, *been* better, and pushed harder! When people give me words of affirmation, this helps remind me that I am noticed, I am enough, and I have done my best. Acts of Service is also a higher category for me because it means that someone else is taking the lead, and I don't have to risk not doing something well or thinking I'll make a mistake.

Gifts and Physical Touch are my two lowest love languages. This might be because I feel as though I'm going to let someone down if I don't like a gift they give me, or that they'll feel as though their gifts are never enough, even though I love them for thinking about me! Physical Touch is my lowest love language because I have a challenging time seeing myself and my body as adequate and sufficient. I even have feelings of rejection about people seeing me naked, and I'm concerned that I don't kiss well enough or that having sex with me is not going to be fulfilling.

This is why I originally wanted to wait to have sex solely with the man I would marry, not only in the sense of knowing that we were both pure to become one as God intended, but also because we would both be new at sex and experience it together. If this is what you want, stay true to it! This standard is countercultural, but doing so will build in you a strength not many others possess. The truth is that I've shown my body in ways I'm not proud of. Shame still tends to come on me full force, especially as I begin a new relationship. I wish I could let it all go! I want to know without a doubt that . . .

I am enough.

I am good enough.

It's okay for me to make mistakes.

It's okay for me to not do something. (This does not make me lazy.)

It's okay that something is out of order.

It's okay to struggle with life, myself, and relationships.

It's okay to be still in God's presence and embrace these growing times because the core of why I'm feeling this is what matters: acceptance.

I pray to embrace my tender heart and weary spirit as I walk with the Lord in this journey of acceptance. I thank God for my life and for the goodness He continues to bring to me daily. I look forward to the day I will get to spend eternity with Him, when "He will wipe every tear from my (their) eyes" Revelation 21:4 (NIV).

There are many resources connected with the Enneagram. I have included a couple of books in the Resource section and highly recommend your reading more about this (understanding, of course, that everyone is different) as a way to better understand not only yourself but also other people. Because these other people include your spouse, partner, family members, children, friends, colleagues and coworkers, and anyone else you encounter.

So, back to it.

I'm an Enneagram One.

I'm a planner.

I'm organized (though I don't always want to be!).

I want people to do the right thing.

I follow the rules.

I'm positive.

I care deeply for others. (Have I mentioned that I'm an empath and a highly sensitive person, too?)

When I'm stressed, I have Enneagram Four tendencies, which means that I feel driven, irrational, and moody and that my self-criticism increases. However, when I'm in a more secure and healthy state (when I feel more relaxed, spontaneous, and playful, and when I'm less critical of myself and able to see beauty in imperfection), I move to Enneagram Seven tendencies.

At the beginning of this shoreline solo adventure, I was in a more stressful state. However, as clarity, strength, compassion, exploration, and going with the flow settled in, I found myself more secure. Although I would love to stay in this secure state all the time, I know that I won't . . . and that's okay. I recognize that my state will ebb and flow! This is what makes life so special.

Old Memories Made New

On the first day of my solo adventure, a friend reminded me to soak up all the little moments and tuck them away for the upcoming school year (and whatever else might be on the horizon). I had this in the back of my mind all week as I soaked up each moment and practiced being present and going with the flow. As I began my fifth day, I woke up not knowing where I'd stay that night but trusting it would all work out—and it did!

Before my last delicious breakfast at Snowbird Inn, I asked on Instagram whether anyone knew of any places to stay in the Traverse City or Petoskey area. I ate breakfast at a table of new people, all connected in some way and all engaged and present in conversation rather than distracted by phones.

After breakfast I went upstairs to pack, reviewed some of the suggestions people had posted, and started my drive to Traverse City to surprise my uncle. However, no such luck. I went to the church he works at and then to his house, but he couldn't be found anywhere. I left him a voicemail and ventured off to Old Mission Peninsula.

My cousin's wife texted me, saying that they were headed to Harbor Springs. They were renting a house for a couple of days, and I would be more than welcome to join them for the night! I had never been to Harbor Springs and had no idea what I was in for. All I knew at that moment was that Old Mission Peninsula was next!

I stopped at 2 Lads Winery and the Mission Point Lighthouse, and then, on my way off the peninsula, decided to make old memories into new ones and stopped at Bonobo Winery. The last time I had been there was with Greg. It was a favorite winery of mine, but was the fascination based on the wine or the remembered company or a little bit of both? We had taken photos together in the vineyard, by the balcony, and by the mural.

There are many wineries in Traverse City and on Old Mission Peninsula. I could have stopped at any of them but chose to make a new memory by stopping at Bonobo. While I was sitting in an Adirondack chair overlooking the vineyard, a ladybug landed on me! I tried to grab my phone to take a photo, but the wind whisked it away! This has become a forever memory, though not reinforced by a photo.

As I wrote in my journal, I reflected on how old memories no longer served me and instead embraced the new ones. The stillness and the breeze sweeping over me reminded me that memories come and go. We can learn from each one and decide how each will affect us and what to do with it. I chose to let the old memories of Bonobo go and to embrace new ones in this setting with open arms, an open heart, and my whole self!

As I pulled away from Bonobo, I thanked God for the time spent there in the past and again in the present. Just as I was leaving Traverse City, my uncle called and told me they weren't in town but were at the Odawa Casino in Petoskey! This was perfect timing, as I would be passing Petoskey in a short while and would make a quick stop to say hi to him and my aunt.

When I arrived at the casino, I was on the lookout for them. I hadn't seen either of them in years, so it was nice to give them a hug and catch up for a bit. My aunt is also my godmother, and I remember her saying, "I can't believe you have been traveling solo lately!" I told her that life is too short not to, to which she replied, "I just want you to be careful, but I also feel like you are living a life I've always dreamed of!" As we said our goodbyes, I told her that it's never too late. I hopped into Turbo, and off I went. Next stop, Harbor Springs!

A Magical Place

I drove through the cute little town, parked, and walked around looking for a place to eat. I had told my cousin and his wife that I wasn't sure what time I'd be at the house but that I'd let them know when I was leaving the restaurant. I certainly wasn't in any rush and wanted to thoroughly enjoy these moments.

I decided to eat at a restaurant on the pier. I told the hostess I'd love to sit outside if there was an open spot at the bar. She checked but told me that they didn't serve food out there. The bartender, though, was wonderful and "snuck" in an order for me! I watched people, ate, and then grabbed a drink to go. Sitting at a picnic table and listening to live music in a nearby park, I noticed a lot of young families with their kids dancing, laughing, and talking. There were also older couples doing the same. It was fun to observe everyone interacting. I felt such a lightness!

While enjoying the park, I looked up the symbolism of a ladybug because they seemed to be showing up regularly on my solo adventure. What I learned brought tears to my eyes: ladybugs are thought to bring good luck, abundance, and protection to all who encounter them. In most European cultures they are seen as an omen of good things to come.

My friend texted me, and I shared what I was doing. She must have told her son, whom I had taught for two years, that we were talking about ladybugs. His question was, "How old were they?" I hadn't even thought about that and was so thankful for a childlike mind to remind me. I didn't know how to figure that out, so I asked him how I could tell. He told me to count the dots. I pulled up the photos I had taken of the ladybugs I had encountered and started counting.

- Ladybug #1 (Glen Arbor): 14 or 15 dots
- Ladybug #2 (Snowbird Inn): 6 or 7 dots
- Ladybug #3 (Bonobo Winery): 2 or 3 dots

I might read too much into things, but it can be beautiful at times to do so. I was about to start my fourteenth year of teaching and was going into my sixth year post Scammer. I wasn't sure about the newest and youngest ladybug but thought its age might mean that it would be two or three years before something big would happen. It's always fun to think a little more deeply about such things. I believe in symbolism and have an awareness of how God moves in my life. These ladybugs mean something to me, just as butterflies do. Both insects have a life cycle that ends in flying free and on their own!

After I was finished writing, I decided to walk the pier before heading to where my cousin was staying. As I walked, I spotted a friend from college with his family; ironically, he happens to be one of Miles's brothers. I gave him a hug, and we chatted for a bit. He introduced me to his wife and his little girls. I wondered if Miles had mentioned anything to his brothers about me when they had been together a short time earlier. We caught up a bit, and I congratulated him on moving away from the city to this quaint, special little town! As we said our goodbyes and I walked away, I thought, *What were the odds of my running into him?* I drove to the house where my cousin and his wife were staying, played a game of Euchre with them, and then went to bed.

The next morning I knew I wanted to spend more time in Harbor Springs. I had no time constraints and told my mom I would let her know when I was on my way to meet them at the lake. I wanted to soak up as much of this charming town as I could. A local coffee shop was first on the list, where I enjoyed a cup of coffee, a muffin, and journaling:

> I just want to take this all in. This week brings tears to my eyes over what I have experienced. The clarity. The strength. The compassion. The flow. What word will today bring as I make my drive back to home base, back to those who raised me, encourage me, and love me unconditionally? What have I learned on this trip?
>
> Everything! When I began this week, I had no idea what it would bring. I went with the flow, wherever my legs, heart, and soul would take me. And because I did this, I am leaving—or, rather, beginning a whole new chapter with my soul full of life. I've found clarity, self-compassion, and strength I wouldn't have found at home! This experience culminates a full year of being single.
>
> A year that has brought growth,
> . . . healing,
> . . . confusion,
> . . . hurt,
> . . . peace, and
> . . . self-acceptance.
> A year that has brought love in a whole new way.
> A love not only for others but for myself.

I finished my coffee, packed up my things, and walked back to my car. As I crossed the street, I peered into a store selling handmade items. I walked in, did a quick look around, and started to walk out; it was then that a display of earrings caught my attention. I picked out a couple of pairs and headed to the register. While standing there, I spotted lotion bars. I asked about them and decided to add one to my purchase. I then saw glass flowers and picked one out each for my mom's rock garden and for my plants. (Those checkout areas, they'll get ya every time!) I added the flowers to my pile before I spotted the rings on display and started looking through them. When I lifted the top tray, there were three more trays of simple but beautiful sterling silver rings. I first put on the classic, plain one, and it fit perfectly. I thought to myself, *I would love a gold one for the top.* However, they didn't have any in my size. So, I asked if all the rings were on display. The lady said, "We have some other 'back-up' ones," at which she pulled them out and looked for a gold band. No luck.

"Did you see the other sterling silver rings in the case over there?" she asked.

"No, I didn't," I responded as I kept looking through the trays. "May I please look at the other container?"

"Absolutely! Look at that, you're the only one in the store! You have it all to yourself!"

I looked around and saw that I truly was the only customer there. I started pulling each ring out of the little squares, and then I saw it.

A ladybug ring!

It was the only one in any of the trays! My fourth ladybug, and the only one I would be able to keep forever! I giggled and asked the lady, "Do you want to hear a story?"

"Sure!" she said.

"I'm on a solo adventure, and I've seen three ladybugs throughout my trip. I just saw my fourth!" I put the ring on my finger, and it fit perfectly! It was as though it had been made just for me!

"It's meant to be!" she exclaimed.

"Yes, it definitely is!"

"I took a solo adventure once and was on the water for a week. No cell phones or anything. It was a long time ago," she shared.

"Where was it at?" I asked.

"In Ohio."

"Nice! I have loved this trip!"

"I came home from that trip, and my life changed and went in a whole different direction."

"Wow! I feel like mine is about to do so as well, after taking this trip. Okay, time to check out with all five of my rings!" I said as I laughed out loud.

As I walked to the register and took off all the rings, the lady started to laugh, too. "Oh, you really do have five!" She started writing them up as I texted a friend what was happening: "I'm shaking! I'm trying to keep it together."

Suddenly another woman, perhaps the owner, came by and said, "This one is on us! I heard your story."

"What? Seriously?" I exclaimed as the tears broke free. "You don't know how much this means to me. Thank you!"

"Oh! You're going to make me cry! Good thing I wore waterproof mascara!"

"May I give you a hug?" I asked.

She came around the counter, and the hug she gave was pure comfort! As I let go, I was in shock and utter amazement! This one person will be part of my story for the rest of my life! As I paid, I looked at both of them and said, "I walked into this store and was about to leave when I stopped and saw the earrings. I never imagined what would happen afterward. This means the world! I can't stop crying! Can I give you another hug?"

"Of course!"

I knew I also wanted to take a photo together.

"Can we also take a photo, please?"

"Yes!"

"I obviously didn't wear waterproof mascara!" I said as we all laughed.

The lady who was helping me with the rings said, "You'll have to send it to Molly."

I looked at the other woman and asked, "What is your name?"

"Molly."

"Oh my gosh! One of my closest friend's name is Molly! This is all just too much! Do you have Instagram?"

"Yes," said Molly as she handed me her card.

With a hand on my heart, I responded, "Thank you! I want you to know that I am writing a book, and you will be a part of it for sure!"

I truly believe this moment was another God wink. This woman, as well as the artist who had created these rings, never knew what a difference they would make on a cloudy, summer day—August 6, 2021! *Thank you* will never do justice as an expression of the peace and true love I felt in this moment. I knew that this was only the beginning of a love for myself that will never be displaced. Instead, it will be protected, guarded, and unforgettable. It will carry me through the days, months, years, and lifetime ahead!

While I had been walking back from Empire Beach on the first day of my trip, the words "Quiet mind . . . Quiet soul" had emerged from my lips and now, as I sat writing on the pier, the ending to those two phrases surfaced:

Quiet mind (*breathe in*).

Quiet soul (*breathe out*).

Loud love.

As I breathed in one last time, I began walking back down the pier. I felt renewed, energized, loved. I felt like myself and didn't ever want to let this feeling go! This spot would re-anchor me. All I needed to do was remember.

As I got into my car and started to drive down Main Street, I recognized that the word that will always describe Harbor Springs for me is *magical*. Harbor Springs will always have a piece of my heart.

The final destination was my parents' lake house. Once there, I eagerly shared all I could and embraced being with them. The next morning, I wrote the following before heading back home:

> The amount of love, joy, peace, and compassion I feel toward myself is something no one will ever understand, but, then again, they don't need to. The timing is perfect as I finish another journal because I'm about to close out another summer and begin year fourteen of teaching. This past year I have grown and healed so much! It has been a year that has included heartbreak, unprecedented times, hurt, tears, and anxiety, but also a lot of joy,

laughter, smiles, appreciation, travels, hope, forgiveness, leadership, and love!

I pray that God will always guide and deliver me from evil and embrace me with unconditional love as He walks beside me on this path of life.

I am proud.

I am proud of myself.

I am proud of how I continue to heal.

I am proud of how I continue to grow.

I am proud of how I am always learning more about who I am, my needs and wants, and the work it has taken, and will continue to take, to get me to my final destination.

I am proud of the love, compassion, and respect I am learning to give myself.

I am proud of learning to set boundaries.

I am proud of my strong body that provides safety, protects, and is the beautiful vessel I have been entrusted to care for, love, and show grace to.

I am proud of where I've been.

I am proud of where I'm going.

I am proud of the love I give so freely.

I am proud of who I am.

I am proud of who I'm becoming.

I am proud.

This lakeshore solo adventure unlocked things in me that I had never before seen. When you unlock something, you open it up.

Think about coming home after a long day at work and unlocking your door, knowing that on the other side is your home, hopefully a safe space where you can move about freely.

Envision opening the fireproof safe where you store your precious documents and memorabilia and being reminded that they are still safe and secure.

Imagine a child pushing open her bedroom door all by herself for the first time and standing there, amazed at the place of freedom she has just entered!

Why are we so afraid to unlock *ourselves*?

Because unlocking ourselves takes vulnerability. It takes courage. It takes knowing that you aren't the only one going through tough times.

Unlocking ourselves can be scary because the unknown always is. But unlocking ourselves can also bring beauty, joy, and freedom that we may never feel if we don't!

Unlocking ourselves lets love in. Love for ourselves, but also for and from others.

Unlocking yourself is a major step toward seeing and accepting the person God created you to be—not just to survive on this earth but to thrive!

Giving yourself permission to unlock yourself is half the battle!

Go ahead.

Here's the key. Unlock yourself!

There are times when unlocking something comes easily and other times when it takes multiple tries. (Take yourself back to middle or high school when you had to figure out how to unlock your locker. My guess is that you didn't get it open on the first try and that this might have caused some stress and anxiety.)

Recall times in your life when unlocking something came more easily and some that were more challenging. Now, dig deeply . . . What parts of you are you still holding back, locking away to prevent others from seeing or hearing?

Create a list of these parts. Once finished, reread your list and circle one aspect of yourself that you want to start unlocking. Think about what steps you might need to take to make this happen. Examples might include:

- Brain dump your thoughts on paper, in a journal, or in a Google or Word document.
- Talk to a trusted friend.
- Schedule a meeting with a therapist or counselor, or research one if you don't have one already.
- Set goals with milestones to celebrate your progress along the way.
- Write down on Post-It notes what you're unlocking and put these notes as reminders in areas you frequently visit.
- Look for and begin reading a blog or book on the topic you desire to unlock.

Once you think about these steps, stand in front of a mirror and repeat these words:

> *I, (insert your name here), give myself permission to unlock this piece of me. It's time to let go. I can and will do this! I'm here to support and love myself along the way. It's time to let love in, and the process starts with me!*

EPILOGUE

Releasing My Story

IT HAS BEEN well over a year since my solo lakeshore adventure, with which I knew I wanted to end my book. It has been an overwhelming task to record and then revise and edit my story to create the book you are reading right now. Fear started to creep in, trying to stop me from moving forward toward putting my love story out into the world. However, through continuous prayer and God's putting people into my life exactly when I needed them, I again overcame fear!

Vulnerability is courageous, and we grow most when we are vulnerable.

2022 has brought me:
Clarity. Purpose. Adventure. Growth. Peace. Closure. Openness.

I was asked one day what I want readers to gain from my story. Initially, I began writing so my readers would know they weren't alone. I felt called to write this book specifically for women, hoping that my words would reach at least one individual in some meaningful way. But I realized that my purpose has expanded. I also want women (everyone, really) to know that we are all broken; we all sin; we all make mistakes; and we all will fail our partners, family members, friends, children, colleagues, and others . . . because we are human. However, it's what we do with all those realities that will truly shape our lives.

My faith and belief in God (*love*) have gotten me through a lot. I want others to hear, read, and be reminded of that as well. The person who asked me the above question responded with, "Interesting how you put love in parentheses after God. To suggest that God *is* love." Yes, I believe He is the ultimate love.

Those who have known me for a while may have noticed other changes. I am the one who looks back and doesn't just notice the changes but *feels* them, too. I've not only changed. I've been transformed. How, you might ask?

- » I see the beauty of the world differently—more clearly and through a different lens.
- » I appreciate seeing a smile, but also sadness, joy, confusion, and hope when looking into someone's eyes.
- » I have learned (and am still learning) that I cannot do it all and that this is okay!
- » I know the importance of leaning in, truly listening, and pausing before trying to "fix" things for myself or someone else, because not all things can be "fixed" right away—it takes time.
- » I'm not alone. Spending time with loved ones and people you meet along the way is precious, irreplaceable, and not to be taken for granted.
- » My wholeness and wellbeing are essential for me to serve and give to others in the way I've been called to.
- » I'm learning to set healthy boundaries, knowing that, though they won't always be welcomed or accepted by others, that's not my problem!
- » I recognize the one life I have to live and the adventures I want to take to make it the fullest life possible.
- » My relationship with God, Jesus, and the Holy Spirit has grown in a way I cannot explain. It's a closeness I know I wouldn't have recognized with all the distractions life was throwing at me prior to COVID.

- We need to experience and endure loss in order to appreciate and enjoy who, and what, has been provided for us.
- I've learned to trust the process. To be even more patient while waiting because the unexpected happens when you're open to receiving it.
- I'm the butterfly who stayed safe in her cocoon for so long, shed the layers through time, and began to expose herself with caution, eventually shaking off the last little bits of debris, while accepting that some will always remain, in order to spread her beautiful wings and fly!

Seasons change.
Both in nature and in life
The sadness may come
But knowing there's a brightness that will prevail
Makes it all worth it.

Remember each season
For what it's brought
    Emotions
    Feelings
    Growth
This season may be coming to an end,
But there's another beautiful one about to bud and blossom!

I wrote this in April 2022 as I began to realize my job was no longer a healthy place for me to be. True colors began to show from the administration, and the support I needed to ensure the safety of my students, fellow colleagues, and myself was not being taken seriously. I was reminded how important my mental, emotional, physical, and spiritual health were and that I was the only one who could protect them. So, I did. I put myself out there in the job market. I had faith in the unknown, trusted in God and in the process, and was patient in the waiting. Not to mention that I had a village behind me every step of the way!

As I closed the door to being a classroom teacher, the dream I'd had since I was five years old, a new one opened as an Early Literacy

Coach. This career would have me supporting and advocating not only for students but for teachers as well. Knowing that this next chapter was about to open for me, I could be free to travel to Europe to explore, recenter, and reconnect to who God had created me to be. And reconnect I did!

In an earlier chapter I shared my dream to travel. One of the biggest adventures I took in 2022 was a solo trip to Europe for thirty days. The adventure started in the airport. I wrote this poem:

Airports
Canceled flights
Loading on and off
Beeps of the scanners
Click, click, click of those who chose to wear heels
Flip, flop of flip flops possibly coming from somewhere warm
  or the reminder of sweet summertime outside.
Have you ever sat and watched people walking to and fro right
  in front of you?
Some at a leisurely stroll
Others at a pace that tells you they are on a mission to make a
  connecting flight.
Fast walk
Light jog
Full on sprint
People of all shapes, sizes, heights, colors, ethnicities, styles
People all with a story
  Some painful
  Some hidden
  Some inspiring
  Some raw
  All their own . . .
    Ready to be told; if they're willing to share and you're
      willing to listen.
Airports are just one of many places where connections
  can be made.

What kind of connections?

Well,

That is up to you to decide!

Within thirty days I explored Portugal, Italy, and Greece, connecting with people who added to and changed my life in some way. Within thirty days I found a new version of myself that I didn't know existed and haven't wanted to lose. I found different parts of myself in each country.

In Portugal, I was reminded to love my neighbor.

I had to remind myself that we all have something to say—and that we say it in many different ways, tones, and expressions. I was also reminded how important it is to take time for myself. That it's okay to go where the night takes me, as long as I remain safe and alert.

In Italy, I fell in love. (This is not what you think.)

There were many times each day that I had a thought or wanted to capture a moment and write it down. Instead, I chose to take a mental picture in the manner that Wendy Speake writes in *The 40-Day Social Media Fast*. I chose to enjoy the moments that presented themselves.

In America, we seem to be always racing from one thing to the next, and I found myself doing so in Italy, too. I found myself walking through the tunnel at a quicker pace than those around me, passing people on the left. But what would my experience have been like if I had paused, stayed behind walkers who were moving at a slower pace, and embraced my surroundings more? I most likely would have seen more children talking and couples holding hands, heard more laughter and tuned in to conversations surrounding me. These were the moments I wanted to bottle up and take with me. I discovered that I could in fact deliberately slow down, and wrote the following:

> I can take the feel of the cool breeze with the hot summer sun beaming down on my golden-brown face.
>
> I can take the sounds of people talking, children screaming and playing, the church bells ringing, and the beautiful melody of Italian being spoken so fluently.

I can take the taste of the fresh bread, cheeses, and meats,
along with the fresh-squeezed juice from Britta's and the
salty taste from the ocean.
I can take the smell of the fried anchovies being prepared,
the freshness of the air surrounding me, and the blooming
flowers all around.
I can see life moving in front of me as people pass by and shops
are opened; the blue expanse and clearness of the sea; the
beautiful, quaint vineyard as I hike; and the creation that
only God could have made for us all to enjoy!
If I could, I would bottle it all up to feel what I'm feeling now—
At peace. Loved. Full of hope and wonder.
Life.

We all get this one life to live. What are we all "waiting" for? The time is now to discover this world, God's beautiful playground, and to notice the love all around us—God's love.

His love found in people who don't speak the same language as us but we both still know what the simple act of smiling can do to form a connection.

His love seen in the flowers, trees, birds, and breeze.

His love, along with life's sentimental daily images, is evident in the laundry hung all around; the local people sweeping off their porches, fixing lunch, and talking with their spouses; a child contented in playing with her toy; and neighbors engaged in conversation. Theirs is a conversation I cannot understand, though I can feel the contentment nonetheless.

I wish I could bottle this part of my adventure because these snippets, taken together, exemplify my story of self-discovery, self-love, acceptance, trust, and truth, not only in myself but in all of humanity. Each of us is one of billions in this world. I know, pray, and hope that I can make a difference no matter where I go, no matter whom I meet along the way or for how long our encounter might last.

In Italy, I fell in love. A special kind of love that so many miss as we adventure through life.

I fell in love with . . .

- » my own breath
- » my own stillness
- » my own peace
- » my own bravery
- » my own resilience
- » my own strength
- » myself!

In Greece, my heart was opened again to let another person in.

Greece had been on my bucket list for the past fifteen years. I didn't know how I would get there or when, but I always felt a slight nudge toward that country. I ended up making another dream come true!

Despite all of my past traumas and relationships, I felt a softness overcome me while in Greece. I was welcomed by Sofia, my Airbnb host, who showed me around town and led me to the most beautiful home-away-from-home, which she called 39 *Steps*, that I got to call my own for a week. I explored Skopelos Island freely, going wherever the day and night took me, with absolutely no plan other than to stay present and alive. I met locals, including Claudio, who showed me places on the island I would never otherwise have known about or been able to explore.

The last night in Skopelos was full of emotion, of desiring to be engulfed in the present moment. I walked the back way to Anatoli's to spend my last night with good food; a beautiful view; calming and comforting music played and sung by Giorgos Xintaris (one of the greatest Greek *rebetes*); and seeing Claudio.

I hugged Claudio on my way out, hoping I would see him one last time when Anatoli's closed for the night. I stood overlooking the beach, listening to the waves crashing on the shore, stargazing, and praying while tears streamed down my face. I was simultaneously feeling all of the emotions as I walked back to 39 *Steps*. Knowing I would have to get up in a few hours, I got ready for bed and crawled in just when Claudio messaged me on Instagram: "Babé girl, where are you?"

I threw on some clothes and went to meet him; he drove to Paralia Glifoneri Beach, right by Sophia's house and Anatoli's. We sat on the rocks looking at the stars, kissing, and talking. I asked Claudio about the meaning of the lyrics sung by Giorgos Xintaris and his sons earlier that evening. Claudio told me they were about the pain, about the love for places one has been. I could feel the degree to which Claudio embraced the lyrics because he sat by the tree where he would often stand and wait, scanning the restaurant and its customers. This evening he seemed to be entranced by the words. The music had been beautiful, and although I hadn't understood the words, I could feel the emotion behind it.

Before we left the beach, Claudio wrapped his arms around me and told me again what a really good time he'd had with me. He wanted me to know—to really believe, how truly special I am! This man, with whom I had spent only three or four days, saw me in a way I truly hadn't seen myself. This was an unexpected gift. Why do I have such a hard time seeing and truly believing in myself? Why do I fight this? Why do I have a hard time hearing it from someone and accepting it? This was the first time I fully and truly saw, felt, and believed in who God had created me to be: beautiful and full of light and love!

Spending time with Claudio, a man who wasn't afraid to say what was on his mind and who carried a genuine confidence in himself, made me realize how much I doubt myself, my intrinsic worth, my not being or feeling adequate or complete. He saw right through it all and told me I needed to stop overthinking and doubting. Claudio opened me up in a way that revealed that it was time for me to recognize these qualities in myself. I'm one person, one woman, who has a lot to offer to this world and to others. I desire to be fully open to everyone and everything that comes my way.

Claudio asked me several times to stop thanking him. But I told him that he needed to know the extent to which he had shown me how to be myself—my smart, carefree, fun, loving, beautiful self. I expressed to him how he had helped me realize how special and one-of-a-kind I am. This man, who came into my life for so short a time, will always be part of my story, of my journey to finding love. For that I thank you, yet again, Claudio. I have a love for Claudio that will always be there because he was part of my journey to help me open my heart to the beautiful woman I am!

My word for 2021 was *courage*.

That was the year I began my solo adventures (Savannah, Scottsdale, and the Lake Michigan shoreline).

My word for 2022 was *adventure*.

That was the year I began a new job and experienced a lifechanging adventure in Europe to discover myself.

When I was in Italy, I came across a cute little wine shop called Ghemé. As the owner helped another customer, I looked at the wincs and found the bottle I wanted right away. The owner ended up telling me the story of the bottle, which was titled *Hope*! Money from each bottle of wine purchased went to support a family who's loved one was battling breast cancer. I chose it because I loved the label and the word on the outside. Knowing the inside story made me love it even more. Little did I know that, six months later, my word for 2023 would be *hope*!

Hope for the present
Hope for the future
Hope for healing
Hope for forgiveness and grace
Hope for joy and happiness
Hope for freedom
Hope for love,
Which I feel in my heart and soul every day.

This journey I've been on has been to find the same love for myself that so many others tell me they see reflected toward others in me. I've longed to truly feel that love and to experience it is an indescribable gift. So many, unfortunately, never discover this type of love. Instead, they rush from one relationship to the next, seeking contentment in other people rather than in God and in who they are as individuals. I have love in my heart. I have love in my soul. I have love to give to others—but also to myself. And I am finally in a place where I don't experience the guilt or shame about doing the next big thing, being this or that, or looking a certain way.

I am simple.
I am beautiful.

I am God's daughter.
I am forgiven.
I am loved.
I am me,
And you are you!

We might think we know—and can orchestrate—our plans, but we really have no clue. God is the One who will work out everything as it's supposed to be. He alone has the full view of our lives from start to finish. We have to choose to trust and follow Him and the way He has mapped out for us every single day (Proverbs 16:3, 9). I am quick to tell you that this is far from easy and that you will need daily reminding because the difficult memories won't ever fully go away. The triggers will come. No matter how hard I try, no matter how much I talk about it, no matter where I'm at, no matter how many sessions with my life coach I have, there will always be events that trigger memories I wish I could forget.

Deep down, however, I know that, if the memories were swept away, this would take away from where I've been and who I am today. This would diminish the impact of my story. I have learned that, the more openly I talk about my experiences and whenever a trigger replays a memory, the easier it has become for me to love and accept myself for the years of punishment, hurt, and heartache I haven't just endured but overcome!

I am thankful for . . .
Time.
Time to love.
Time to rest.
Time to heal.
Time to grow.
Time to forgive.
Time to cherish.
Time to make mistakes.
Time to move forward.
Time to laugh.
Time to cry.

Time with God.
Time with loved ones.
Time to remember to take it one step, one day,
one minute at a time.

I look back on the life I've lived thus far. I know there is a reason for everything God has put into my life and the way He guides me through every moment. There has been, and always will be, an overarching reason for His timing, even if we don't see it right away (Jeremiah 29:11–14). All we have is today. So the question is, how are you living today?

My prayer is that, even while reading my story, you have remembered your own story and recognized and appreciated how loved you are. So, sit in the silence, grow through the uncomfortable, and find joy in the morning. It's because of your past and in your hope for the future that you get to live in the present and feel fully alive!

Put your hand on your heart. Yes, right now.

Take a breath and be patient as you wait.

Do you hear it?

Do you feel it?

It's your beating heart, reminding you of how alive you are.

It's your beating heart, reminding you that there is a reason you have gone through everything you have.

My love story was never about finding another person to "complete" me. Only God can do that. My love story is about taking the time and choosing to unlock parts of myself that kept me captive for so long. Writing my love story has been healing and freeing. Releasing my love story into the world will bring a new kind of freedom. I know it is my time. I know I am ready to be fully set free to *soar* into the life God has called me to live! I am forever grateful.

Be vulnerable.
Be courageous.
Be true to who you are.
Unlock the love you have within.
Be set free!

RESOURCES

Books Mentioned:

Eat, Pray, Love by Elizabeth Gilbert
Eat, Pray, #FML by Gabrielle Stone
The Meaning of Marriage by Timothy Keller
The Ten Best Days of My Life by Adena Halpern
You're Already Amazing by Holley Gerth
Jesus Calling by Sarah Young
The Body Keeps the Score by Bessel van der Kolk
Think Again by Adam Grant
Crucial Conversations by Joseph Grenny, Kerry Patterson, Ron McMillan, Al Switzler, and Emily Gregory
The 7 Rocks of Life: The Key to Filling Up Your Life Cup by Steven Mazzurco
The Gifts of Imperfection by Brené Brown
The Four Agreements: A Practical Guide to Personal Freedom (A Toltec *Wisdom Book)* by Don Miguel Ruiz
The Road Back to You by Ian Morgan Cron and Suzanne Stabile
Growing as an Enneagram One (60-Day Enneagram Devotional) by Elisabeth Bennet (There are other books based on each Enneagram number.)
The 5 Love Languages: The Secret to Love That Lasts by Gary Chapman
The 40-Day Social Media Fast by Wendy Speake

Additional Books:

Unraveled: Unravel, Uncover, and Reveal Your Beauty by Rachel Williams

Love Defined: Embracing God's Vision for Lasting Love and Satisfying Relationships by Kristen Clark and Bethany Baird

7 Myths about Singleness by Sam Allberry

Thank You for Rejecting Me: Transform Pain into Purpose and Learn to Fight for Yourself by Kait Warman

Love in Every Season: Understanding the Four Stages of Every Healthy Relationship by Debra Fileta

Podcasts:

Better! with Dr. Stephanie
Time and Energy Management for Ambitious Women

Love and Relationships with Debra Fileta

Space & Purpose with Sara Gonzalez

Unlocking Us with Brené Brown

Websites:

Research about nonverbal communication from Albert Mehrabian:
https://online.utpb.edu/about-us/articles/communication/how-much-of-communication-is-nonverbal/

Mental Health:

The JED Foundation
https://jedfoundation.org/resource/mental-health-warning-signs-and-when-to-ask-for-help/

National Alliance on Mental Illness (NAMI)
https://www.nami.org/About-Mental-Illness

Verywell Mind
https://www.verywellmind.com/

Healthline
https://www.healthline.com/mental-health

ACKNOWLEDGMENTS

God: You never said this life would be easy. In fact, you said there would be trials and tribulations along the way, and you promised to be right there with me through everything. Thank you for holding true to your endless promises, for protecting me, and for showing me what you have seen in me since before I was born.

Mom and Dad: No matter where life has taken me, you have been by my side supporting me, encouraging me, drying my tears, driving to visit, endless hugs, laughing, listening, and loving me every day of my life. I thank God for making me your daughter and into the caring, independent woman you have raised me to be.

Michelle: I thank God every day for you. For your limitless amounts of coaching, love, support, and encouragement. Everyone needs people in their corner, and you were, and still are, an intricate part of my healing journey. I wouldn't be where I am today without your willingness to meet me that evening on June 29, 2016. Totally a God-send!

Friends: There are too many to express my gratitude to all of you. One gift God has given me is to connect with people and cherish relationships and quality time with friends. Thank you to all who knew me growing up, for all who were with me through being catfished and the aftermath of healing, for all of those I have met along the way, and for those I have yet to meet. I love the quote, "People come into your life for a reason, a season, or a lifetime." No matter which category you fall into, I am thankful our paths have crossed.

Previous Relationships: It's because of you that I am the woman I am today. Thank you for the memories, the tears, the laughter, and the amount of time I have given myself to heal and move forward from each of you. It's because of you that I get to appreciate the growth I have undergone, what I continue to learn about myself and others, and the gift that singleness has brought me.

My Publishing Team: From meeting Susie Finkbeiner in a short-term small group at Ada Bible Church to our two-hour long conversation about what publishing a book entails to her connecting me with Ann Byle, my book coach, and coming full circle to working with Tim Beals at Credo House Publishing, thank you! Thank you for coaching, supporting, and encouraging me through this book publishing process. Your commitment to seeing me through and reminding me to trust the process is exactly what I needed to keep going!

My Readers: Thank you for taking the time to read my story but, more importantly, to reflect on your own. You are one of the many reasons I wrote this book for the world to read. I pray you remember how important it is to unlock yourself and what a gift it is to be alive!

ABOUT THE AUTHOR

STACEY SZCZEPANSKI is a resilient, empathetic, highly sensitive, and vulnerable woman. She is a woman of faith and continues to grow her relationship with Jesus daily. Stacey is passionate about spending time with and learning from other believers, educators, and singles. Stacey lives in West Michigan, where she can often be found exploring God's beautiful playground and spending quality time with her family and friends. She also enjoys traveling to different parts of the world, journaling, taking naps, spending time at local coffee shops, and sipping wine with friends. She looks forward to connecting with you!

- Website: StaceySzczepanski.com
- Instagram: @StaceySzczepanski
- Facebook: Facebook.com/Stacey.Szczepanski.9

Made in United States
Orlando, FL
15 June 2024